HOW TO
Win
· IN A ·
CRISIS

CREATH DAVIS

HOW TO
Win
· IN A ·
CRISIS

PYRANEE
BOOKS

Zondervan Publishing House
Grand Rapids, Michigan

How to Win in a Crisis
Copyright © 1976 by Creath Davis

Pyranee Books are published by Zondervan
Publishing House, 1415 Lake Drive, S.E.,
Grand Rapids, Michigan 49506

Library of Congress Cataloging in Publication Data
Davis, Creath
    How to win in a crisis.

    Includes bibliographical references.
    1. Pastoral psychology. 2. Interpersonal relations.
I. Title.
BV4012.D346   248'.4   76-42200
ISBN 0-310-23191-4

Printed in the United States of America

87 88 89 90 91 92 / CH / 11 10 9 8 7 6 5 4

To our parents
Vernon and *Treva Davis*
Laura Mae Watson,
and the late *Eldred Watson,*
who have given us much

Contents

Foreword by Gloria and Bill Gaither
Preface
Acknowledgments

PART ONE — HANDLING PERSONAL CONFLICTS

PART TWO — CONFRONTING CONFLICT IN
RELATIONSHIPS

Foreword

In a world of easy answers to hard problems, glib lists of quick, painless solutions to nearly everything, and avalanches of self-help treatises on how to succeed, succeed, succeed — it is refreshing to find such a manual as Creath Davis's new help for strugglers.

Perhaps it would be best to say at the outset that if you've never failed, never known defeat, never found unbearable loss, never had to sew the garment of life from the fabric of "less-than-best," this book is not for you. But for those who are searching for the joy that comes from seeing "God's power show up best in weak people" when *you* are the "weak people," read on!

In our success-oriented society it is a delight also to invite you into the Family of God, the only group where you have to lose everything to even get in — the only fellowship in which you can fail without being a failure. "He that would lose his life for my sake," said Jesus, "shall find it."

We have a feeling that one of the main reasons this book was written was to help those who are standing in the rubble of shattered dreams, broken health, crushed aspirations, and personal defeats to pick up the pieces, "wrap them all in the rags of their lives and lay them at the cross."

So, welcome to the losers, who have lost it all to find *everything!*

GLORIA and BILL GAITHER

Preface

This book is an outgrowth of nearly twenty years of trying to relate the good news of the Christian faith to the practical needs of people. The experience that motivated me to write under the title *How to Win in a Crisis* came from a men's sharing group. During the year that we met, every man in that group faced one or more of the biggest crises of his life. The pressures were real, but so were the resources of their faith. I witnessed again the power of the living Christ who enables us to change our weaknesses into strengths, our failures into successes, and our crises into opportunities for discovery and growth.

The design of this book is simple. It is written for busy people in the thick of life. It is intended to serve as a *way-pointer* and not as an exhaustive treatise on the thirty subjects covered. When we face a severe crisis, the first few steps we take in attempting to deal with the situation are the most critical. The sooner we begin moving in a creative direction, the sooner we can come to grips with the reality before us and find adequate resources for dealing with that reality. *How to Win in a Crisis* calls your attention to these dynamic resources which are available to us all.

A word about how to read this book is in order. You will probably begin with the chapter that relates most clearly to your specific need or interest. That is certainly justifiable. However, there are insights throughout which will relate directly or indirectly to your life experiences. In other words, this book is a cohesive unit and not a collection of unrelated material. Take for example the chapter "Living With an Alcoholic." You may not be living with an alcoholic or be closely associated with someone who has a severe drinking problem; but there are insights that will help you understand yourself and others much more than the chapter title would lead you to believe. Moreover, the likelihood of your having to deal eventually with alcoholism in someone you know increases daily.

If you are looking for easy answers to tough problems, forget this book. If you are looking for some workable answers which are not "pat," then try it.

CREATH DAVIS

Acknowledgments

An adequate acknowledgment is impossible. So many people have shared both their dreams and their struggles with me in retreats, Bible study groups, counseling sessions, and a continuing fellowship called Christian Concern which have influenced not only my writing, but also my life. This book is a witness of hope from this community — a Living Hope embodied in Jesus Christ!

Without the efforts of my wife, Verdell, who listened and labored with me in the writing of this book; Gwynne Pollock, who gave countless hours to editing; and Norma Atlason, my secretary, who typed and retyped this manuscript, this book would never have come to fruition.

A special thanks to the directors of Christian Concern, who have been more of a family than an official board for us — George and Ann Clark, John and Sybil Allison, Dan and Martha Lou Beaird, George and Miley Busiek, Roy and Janis Coffee, Charles and Gwen Davis, Don and Mary Ann Edney, Parker and Lois Folse, Charley and Aggie Johnson, Tommy and Patricia Jones, Ray and Sharon Powell, Johnny and Patsy Jones, John and Frances Saville, Dan and Jimmie Abbott — and to the larger body of the Christian Concern fellowship.

And thanks to our staff at Kaleo Lodge who have modeled for us a servant community and have certainly influenced the shape of this book — R. C. and Kay Blackstock; Billie Jean, Cindy, and Brad Hepp; Latrell and Mary Bryant — and to John Hepp, author and teacher, who leads a weekly Bible study at the Lodge.

A Word of Thanks

To the men's sharing group, comprising several of the directors named above and Tex Williams, Larry Fleck, Mike McCullough, and David Burgher, where the idea for this book was born;

For fellowship and sharing:

Martin and Karen Cude, Weldon and Brenda Shelton, Tom and Ruth Randall, Al and Sue Simmons, Hal and Mary Lynn Mayfield, Bob and Susan McLendon, Bill and Boyce Byers, David and Litty Turner, Dean and Patsy Coppage, John B. Kidd, and Mr. and Mrs. D. L. Riley;

For special contributions:

Robert A. Williams, who has helped me in every facet of this ministry, including the writing of this book;

Carmen and Dorothy Conner, who pointed the way toward invaluable research for this project, along with George Roberts, my supervisor for the American Association of Marriage and Family Counselors;

Glenn Reddell and staff members and constituency of the Spiritual Growth Foundation in Lubbock, Texas, who have helped me focus more clearly on specific areas of need in a community ministry;

Bill and Gloria Gaither who gave me the opportunity to present the contents of this book in seminar form at the "Praise Gathering for Believers" in Indianapolis, Indiana, in November 1975;

Bob DeVries and Al Bryant of Zondervan Publishing House, who have encouraged me in each of my writing projects.

James E. Ruark, Manuscript Editor at Zondervan, who has worked enthusiastically on this project with me.

The following Scripture versions are quoted with grateful acknowledgment to their publishers:

PART ONE

Handling Personal
Conflicts

Don't just pretend that you love others: really love them. Hate what is wrong. Stand on the side of the good. Love each other with brotherly affection and take delight in honoring each other. Never be lazy in your work but serve the Lord enthusiastically. Be glad for all God is planning for you. Be patient in trouble, and prayerful always. When God's children are in need, you be the one to help them out. And get into the habit of inviting guests home for dinner or, if they need lodging, for the night.

If someone mistreats you because you are a Christian, don't curse him; pray that God will bless him. When others are happy, be happy with them. If they are sad, share their sorrow. Work happily together. Don't try to act big. Don't try to get into the good graces of important people, but enjoy the company of ordinary folks. And don't think you know it all!

Never pay back evil for evil. Do things in such a way that everyone can see you are honest clear through. Don't quarrel with anyone. Be at peace with everyone, just as much as possible.

Dear friends, never avenge yourselves. Leave that to God, for He has said that He will repay those who deserve it. [Don't take the law into your own hands.] Instead, feed your enemy if he is hungry. If he is thirsty give him something to drink and you will be "heaping coals of fire on his head." In other words, he will feel ashamed of himself for what he has done to you. Don't let evil get the upper hand but conquer evil by doing good.

— Romans 12:9-21
The Living Bible

> *Life is like walking through the snow —*
> *every step shows.*
>
> — *Jess Lair*

1. How Do You React to Conflict?

"CAN YOU BELIEVE what has happened to me? You've seen me down and desperate. And I am here to tell you that nothing has changed at home. Our marriage may even be in worse shape than before. But I am coping with the situation now in a way I never dreamed possible."

That was good news from a friend who had come to me for help in her desperate hours. Everything was not okay, but she was, and that made a remarkable difference.

Sure, we would all prefer that our problems go away or, better yet, never appear. But even the smartest and the strongest will one day find that life has moved beyond his control. The awareness of such vulnerability usually shocks us into disbelief: "I can't believe this is happening to me." And the way we respond to this shattering experience will either open new dimensions of growth or strangle every ounce of energy from our spirit. If we want to remain *alive* for the full duration of our years, we must discover how to survive courageously and creatively the crises that inevitably come.

19

We are defining *crisis* as "anything that forces change." The more radical the change, the more intense the experience. Adolescence brings greater conflict than the earlier stages of childhood, because the changes occurring are more extreme. The struggle to become one's own person carries greater pain than simply submitting to the care of another. The equipment we have and the response we make in any given crisis determine the effect that it will have upon us.

The fluid nature of personal relationships demands changes from time to time that may precipitate a crisis of one degree or another. The change demanded may arise out of a strained or disintegrating relationship between husband-wife, parent-child, employer-employee, in-laws, or friends. Something happens, and we become painfully aware that all is not well in the relationship. Our reactions to such relational desperation are varied.

1. A common response to personal conflict is simply to deny that a problem exists and play the "everything's great" game. An indication of such reaction is the need to declare repeatedly to others how great things really are. Inwardly we are simply trying to convince ourselves, but the conflict only intensifies with this approach.

One couple sharing part of their struggle with me is battling this process of denying reality. A relationship that began with great promise has been crippled because of an unwillingness on the part of one to admit that a problem exists. *We seem to forget that a mark of true strength is one's ability to admit weakness.* In making the transition from sex being exciting because of its newness to the richer expression of sex being exciting because of the deepening relationship of married love, this couple ran into difficulty. The husband fell victim to the "get ahead in business at any price" syndrome while the wife rushed headlong into the social arena. The goal of one seemed to complement the goal of the other nicely, but along the way they lost each other. Some of us could probably identify with this couple if we substituted reputation, children, pleasure, or success in any one of a hundred different ways as the thing that lured us from the priority of really learning how to love the person we married.

The day came when the wife, feeling unloved, withdrew sexually. The husband wanted her, but did not know how to woo her back. A tug of war developed around their sexual relationship. The wife, seeking to defend herself, attacked his masculinity; her tactics were very effective, causing her husband to withdraw from her and move into a world of sexual fantasy. His withdrawal frightened her, and she overcompensated by moving toward him as the sexual aggressor; this demolished the last thread of masculinity for him.

Feeling hostile and helpless, he sought counsel from a psychiatrist. The very act of allowing an understanding person in on this crazy thing that was happening to him brought both relief and hope. When he tried to enlist his wife in the counseling process, however, she refused. "There's nothing wrong with me, and there's nothing wrong with you either. We don't need any help" was her comment. This reaction increased their alienation to the extent that all they had left were resentments and criticism. The best solution that they could adopt was for each to go his own way but retain their marital status for the children's sake.

Once a relationship disintegrates to this degree, it becomes a live bomb needing little to cause detonation. This conflict is far from being resolved, but the first major step toward health for one has been taken — willingness to admit the presence of the problem. This does not guarantee that the relationship will survive, but it does offer new possibilities in the way the husband may react in the situation. And when the changes occurring open new insight and freedom for one, the chances for a healthy response from the other increase enormously.

2. Another common response in a relational crisis is to cast the blame for the problem on someone else. We sometimes call this projection — projecting the source of the conflict away from ourselves. We may not be willing or able to deal with our own failure in the relationship, so we dump it all on the other person and feel very pious about what we have done. After all, we have located the *real* problem. Human nature has this bent to a remarkable degree.

"If he would just spend one day doing my job, he might realize how important I am to this company." "If my in-laws only knew how spoiled and selfish their son is, maybe they would stay off my back." "If my parents were not so demanding, perhaps I would have more respect for them. After all, I am a good guy, and there would not be any conflict in our relationship if *they* would straighten up and fly right." "They" are always the culprits in this response pattern. "They" can be a spouse, a parent, an employer, or the federal government. But regardless of who "they" are, *they* are to blame!

This negative response pattern is modeled for us in the first relational conflict man ever encountered. Adam and Eve in the Garden of Eden ate the forbidden fruit. This was a violation of both trust and the command of God. They previously had enjoyed perfect harmony and fellowship with their Creator, but after this act of defiance they hid themselves. Now, try as we will, there are two persons we cannot avoid forever — God and ourselves. The record reveals that in the ensuing encounter Adam faced not only God but himself as well. God called, "Adam, where are you?" What a profound question! "Where are you in the garden? Where are you in our relationship? Where are you in relation to yourself? to your helpmate?"

Adam's response is as profound. "I heard your voice and was afraid." Afraid of what? "Afraid because I was naked. Where am I? I am naked — ashamed, guilty, afraid, exposed, alienated. So I hid myself."

How many times have we tried to cover our tracks, hide ourselves, because we too were afraid, guilty, ashamed, alienated? The only adequate way out of such dilemma is to reach beyond ourselves to God's grace and forgiveness, readily available in Jesus Christ.

But not Adam! Instead of dealing squarely with his guilt, he cast the blame elsewhere. His scapegoats became the others in his world. First, the blame belonged to Eve ("She gave me the fruit"), but the ultimate blame belonged to God ("He gave me the woman").

The desire to escape responsibility for our own actions is incredible. We seem to feel subconsciously, if not consciously, that if we can turn the table just enough to include God in our blame-scale, then we have a way of dealing with Him and retaining unapologetically our own self-centered life-style. But all existence bears witness to the fact that self-centeredness carries its own guarantee of destruction, and to block one's self from God is to cut off the precious flow of creative life.

Blaming others for our struggle is so unproductive that it can blind us to any alternative which might help. We are left with the feeling of being trapped and at the mercy of fate. I do not wish to trigger in those with supersensitive consciences the other extreme of assuming all the guilt in the situation. We need to accept our share, but never the whole. This pattern is seen often in divorces: moving from blaming the other to taking all the blame ourselves. At first we may be all too eager to lay the blame on our spouse. "It is all her fault (or his fault). I did everything possible to make a good marriage but she (or he) failed to carry her (or his) share of the relationship." After this stage, however, usually comes the "I failed" stage. "If I had been more sensitive to her (or his) needs, if I had tried harder, if I had gotten adequate help when the marriage began to fall apart, if . . . if . . . if . . ."

It is true, no doubt, that more blame belongs to one of the two involved. *But the failure is mutual!* What we discover about our own faults and those of our spouse can give us some understanding about both our needs and theirs, but to become locked either in self-hate or bitterness is again to be trapped in a self-destructive pattern.

It is good to be reminded that one failure, even if it is the biggest one we can conceive, does not of itself doom us to a life of failure. Allowing ourselves to think otherwise poisons the spirit and depresses the mind, leaving only a sense of utter hopelessness. A person in this state feels as if he has no future, nothing to look forward to; his life holds no promise. Recurring depression becomes the norm and will continue unless this negative emotional pattern can be broken.

3. Another common malady in relational crisis is the effort to deal with the conflict superficially. The offender may offer the "let's just forget the whole matter and go on" solution without any basis for either forgetting or going on. The result of such action would simply be to bury the problem by blocking it out of the mind. At best, any relief would be only temporary. The things we bury before they

are dead always come back to haunt us. Furthermore, seldom is the offended party willing to forget the offense without some basis for doing so.

Our first attempts to resolve difficulties are usually superficial. It seems to be a universal fact that we are willing to change only when we are convinced there is no other way.

I am presently involved in a counseling situation that dramatically demonstrates the case in point. Mary has just found out after fifteen years of marriage that along with Ray's apartment in Chicago is a mistress. It is an understatement to say that Mary's world has been shattered. She loves Ray and has tried from her perspective to be everything he needs.

Being the vice-president of a large company with headquarters in Chicago and living in Dallas, Ray has had to be away from home a great deal. Two years ago he leased an apartment to save on expenses, so he told Mary. But with the apartment came another woman.

Mary was battling her own loneliness to give Ray the freedom for travel that she felt his company demanded. But now she feels like a complete fool. Over the past two years Ray has gradually withdrawn all physical affection from her while continuing to assure her verbally of his love. Mary thought he was having a problem with impotency, and she was committed to nursing him back to health. Then to discover that what he was withholding from her was being given to another — well, that was too much! Hurt and enraged, she tried to kill him. Ray took the gun away from her and tried to explain that the affair was over even before she found out about it. The solution he has offered to Mary is "Forget the whole thing and let's go on as before." The most naive of us would recognize that there must be more involved in the restoration of this relationship than Ray has offered. And I think Mary has about convinced him that there is a need for more than a superficial solution to the problem.

Attacking the wrong problem never resolves the real one. Each one of us has a list of emotionally safe, acceptable problems and of dangerous, unacceptable ones. Every time one of these dangerous, unacceptable problems begins to appear we will be tempted to substitute a more acceptable one with which to struggle. The majority of the people who have come to me for counseling have presented a problem to be resolved which was not *the* problem at all.

In a retreat at Kaleo Lodge a very prominent man asked for a private conference: he said his vocational direction concerned him. After two hours of building trust and digging deeper into the situation, I saw the real issue emerge. It came as a surprise to him! His father at age seventy-five still held tightly the reins of their company. The son was never asked his opinion or included in the decision-making process, even though he held the title of the No. 2 man in the company. At forty he had submitted to total domination as long as he could. His resentment was deep and ready to explode. But this feeling was so unacceptable to his conscious mind that he had channeled his frustration in another direction. He could accept a vocational problem, but not a relational one with his father.

There is no doubt that it would be easier for this man to change companies than to change his relationship with his father. But for his sake as well as his father's, there must be an honest sharing of feelings before a parting of the ways is even considered. I have seen major miracles transpire when individuals have openly shared their feelings in similar situations. Usually the one dominating does not have even an inkling that there is a problem. He may not intend to squeeze the other person out of anything, but is himself so aggressive that he will have to make a conscious effort to include others.

There are times, however, when the dominant person may be so threatened by this kind of confrontation that a detachment will be the only door open for freedom. But the confrontation will reduce the need for resentment, and their parting can be as peers. They may not be able to work together now, but they have faced their quandary and taken some decisive action in it. This struggle is akin to the parent-adolescent struggle and holds the same possibilities for good or ill.

Giving another person gifts instead of giving one's self leaves much to be desired in working out adequate relationships. This can occur in any relationship, but seems to be predominant in the parent-child relationship. Our children from their birth are *little people* who grow very rapidly into *big people*. As parents, it is easy to get caught in the providing-for-them syndrome and forget that our children have needs and rights as human beings. Since parents provide the physical necessities of life, it is natural to assume that the emotional and spiritual needs are being met as well. After all, your love is being expressed in preparing a meal or doing laundry. True! But is your love also revealed in listening, taking seriously both the verbal and nonverbal messages being sent by the child?

The child can feel that his relationship to his parents is bent out of shape. How can he resolve that conflict unless his parents are willing really to be with him — to see his world as he sees it, to feel what he feels? It is easier to buy him a toy and send him into the other room to play than to go into that room yourself and be his gift.

Frequently when a parent's guilt level is raised by an incident in which he did not deal lovingly with his child, he may give him something to avoid saying, "I am sorry." But if we could remember that our children are people who need people, just as we, and respond to them the way we would like the most significant person in our lives to respond to us — well, the results would be fantastic for everyone involved.

We have examined some common responses to personal conflict that are inadequate for the continued health of either the individual persons or the relationship. We have had to resist the temptation to focus our attention on the obvious faults of the other person or persons in our own relational crisis. Their faults are much easier to see than our own. But the question is, can we identify our own weak reactions and concentrate our energy on health-evoking changes within ourselves?

Questions for Personal Reflection and Group Interaction

1. What motivated you to read this book or to participate in this group?
2. What needs are you bringing to this experience?
3. Are you looking for answers for yourself or for someone else?
4. On which side of the ledger would you place yourself today — the okay side or the not-okay side?
5. On which side of the ledger would you place the other person or persons involved in your conflict — okay or not okay?

6. Have you ever had a shattering experience? What was it? What did you do?
7. Have you ever knowingly tried to deny that a problem existed, hoping that the denial itself would cause it to go away?
8. How hard is it for you to face up to your own weaknesses?
9. Have you ever felt the need to blame another for your problem?
10. Are you aware of dealing with any conflicts superficially?
11. How do you manage your personal conflicts?

2. Creative Relationships Do Not Happen Accidentally

IT IS BEYOND OUR power to change others directly. We can exert tremendous influence by our actions and attitudes, but the autonomy of the other guarantees his freedom to respond to us and to life as he alone chooses. This capacity for self-direction is one of God's great gifts to human beings. It is not, however, a gift we necessarily accept wholeheartedly. It carries with it not only incredible opportunity, but also sobering responsibility for oneself.

In a very real sense we are what we choose to be! There are experiences that push us in self-defeating directions, but these experiences do not in themselves determine what we shall become. Should we choose to be carried along by the wind of circumstance, we will be molded by those circumstances. But within each of us lies the potential for swimming upstream and becoming more than our environment dictates.

The greatest danger in surrendering our autonomy is that we make ourselves totally dependent upon others for our sense of well-being. Then we become susceptible to the product of whatever emotional immaturity they may possess.

28

The goal for human relationships is not dependence or independence, but interdependence. Interdependence allows each person to stand on his own feet and give what he has to give with no strings attached. He is also free to receive what the other offers, but is not driven to demand more. This balance is the ideal which we must pursue, but which we will never fully possess. It is certain that unless we move toward definitive goals in our relationships, we will inevitably repeat the same mistakes again and again.

What are some objectives for developing meaningful relationships? *Mutual respect* must be first. It is painfully obvious to us when we do not receive respect, yet our failure to hold another in esteem can easily slip past our consciousness. Since our prejudices are ours, they seem normal and right. But to be on the wrong end of someone's "normal" prejudices can be devastating.

It is not uncommon to discover that the underlying problem which has destroyed a family is the loss of mutual respect. How easy it is to lose sight of the beauty we first discovered in our differences. The complementary components of the husband-wife relationship offer possibilities for fulfillment which no other relationship can equal. In spite of this initial allure we can become easily sidetracked into trying to make our spouse over in our own image — seeing his strengths as threats and his weaknesses as inadequacy. Instead of helping, we *attack* or *withdraw*, leaving the other bruised and uncertain about where he stands in our affections. Such action usually calls forth retaliation of one kind or another, and the war (cold or hot) begins. The ensuing battle may obliterate any desire to recognize or evoke the good in the other. Unchecked, this response pattern can demolish all respect and leave the relationship hopelessly crippled.

A good friend shared part of his journey that illustrates the need to respect and affirm the uniqueness of one's spouse. He grew up shy. But as a young man he was attracted to a vivacious, outgoing girl. She was everything he was not, and he liked the contrast. He emerged from his shyness long enough to court and win this girl as his bride. Then, he says, he spent the next fifteen years trying to change his wife — trying to change the very things that had first attracted him to her. His efforts caused them both great pain.

In a retreat something happened which opened the door to a new beginning for this couple. Religion had always been an activity they participated in because it was proper. But during that weekend of sharing and examining the good news of the Christian faith they decided to commit themselves to Jesus Christ as God's revelation of Himself and as their personal Savior. The freedom and love they experienced created a deeper awareness of and love for each other. This man has been able to affirm his wife in a beautiful way, and the respect they share for one another has enriched me and everyone else who has been touched by their lives.

We all have our particular sensitivities and preferences, which are a valid part of being human. But measuring the worth of another person on the basis of our own partiality can impoverish us by shutting out the possibility of significant relationships with that large segment of humanity that differs from us socially, economically, and generationally.

We do have a class system in our culture that runs as deep as racism and can be every bit as destructive. I have seen many individuals hurt deeply by the social lines drawn within our "melting pot" culture. Many find ways to build walls around themselves and their crowd to keep those who are not "in" out. Being "in" becomes a mark of distinction and superiority. This separative social system violates a basic premise of the Christian faith. "Show no partiality as you hold the faith of our Lord Jesus Christ."[1] "For God has no favourites."[2] "For now that you have faith in Christ Jesus you are all sons of God. . . . Gone is the distinction between Jew and Greek, slave and free man, male and female — you are all one in Christ Jesus."[3]

Even apart from the Christian faith, such bias blocks any possibility for social cohesiveness and wholesomeness. A disturbing element on the contemporary scene in America is the reaction occurring from years of deep-seated prejudice. People are choosing sides and demanding of society their "place in the sun." But the direction this revolt has taken is the attempt to change the recipients of preferential treatment rather than build a system of equality. To survive as a nation we must break this vicious social attitude of putting down those who are not like us and give ourselves intently to understanding the anxious, frustrated, lonely people in our midst. It is not strange that the truth the Christian gospel offers is the only real solution for a lasting society. One part of that gospel emphatically teaches that only in seeking to meet the needs of others can we find our own needs being met.

It is true that we are not all equal in gifts, opportunities, education, experience, or any of a hundred other specific qualities we might name. Neither do we make equal contributions to the welfare of the human race. However, we are equal in the matter of human worth and responsibility. We have been made in the image of God with unbelievable potential and with the freedom to direct the unfolding of that potential for good or ill. Francis Schaeffer stated the case clearly when he wrote,

> With God there are no little people. . . . Our attitude toward all men should be that of equality because we are common creatures. We are of one blood and kind. As I look across the world, I must see every man as a fellow creature and I must be careful to have a sense of our equality on the basis of this common status. We must be careful in our thinking not to try to stand in the place of God to other men. We are fellow creatures.[4]

As men our major challenge is to make the most of what we have been given. Consequently the greater our gifts, the greater our responsibility. Yet the thrust of the Christian message is always that the greater serves the lesser. This pattern is the only one in which mutual respect can emerge between super-achievers and low-achievers, or between any other opposites on the scale of human characteristics. Otherwise, the stronger exploits the weaker, and the weaker hates the stronger for it. No relationship can survive the loss of respect.

Another clear objective for a significant relationship is a commitment to calling forth the good in the other. Such activity releases the best in us as well. The stimuli we bring to bear on those with whom we interact either encourages or discourages the development of their own unique selves. It is incredible how much negative input bombards most people in the course of a single day.

One simple example happened recently. While waiting for an attendant to service my car, two workmen stopped by the station for gas. Another customer who knew the workmen made the sarcastic remark, "Aren't you two going to do any work today? It's almost noon, you know." It was no friendly joke. The two workmen said yes and went on their way. One more shower of bad news for two men who obviously were already on the job. A day of belittling remarks takes its toll on the strongest of men. And I wonder how they will respond to their wives and children in the evening?

How can we break our negative response patterns? By starting with our attitudes! How do you feel about people in general? How do you feel about yourself? Are you worth paying attention to in your own mind? What kind of commitment do you have with regard to your relationship with others? Are you a "don't bother me" type, a "get out of my way" type, a "don't expect anything from me" type, an "I never saw you" type, or hopefully a "welcome into the family of the human race" type? All except the last inevitably lead to loneliness.

It does no good to settle in self-pity over all the negative material given us. We need to make a commitment to ourselves and others that the underlying conviction of our lives will be that *all are important*. To think of ourselves and others as "unique, unrepeatable miracles of God" lays a solid foundation from which we can begin to call forth the exciting potential in others.

Verdell and I have been married fifteen years. To some that sounds like forever, while to others we may be beginners. Regardless of where we are on your time scale, the thing that absolutely astounds me is the continued discovery of new sensitivities and beauty in her that I never dreamed of. She has always been a beautiful person and lover to me, but I find that the more we share, the more we discover who we are and who the other is. That is exciting! Verdell's father died recently. I saw coming out of that experience a new strength in her which I joyously affirm and celebrate with her. The way she has been able to experience her grief — feeling the loss very deeply and accepting the reality of death as part of the life process — and to come to a quiet faith through it all has opened new depths in all her relationships.

There are many ways we can communicate a sense of worth to another person. Bob Slocum tells the story of a family eating

out one evening with five-year-old Junior. The parents gave their
order to the waitress and proceeded to order for Junior. The little boy
blurted out that he wanted a *hamburger*; the waitress listened and
asked what he wanted on it. He told her, and as she was leaving, the
little boy excitedly announced to his parents, "The lady thinks I'm
real!" Her taking the order from Junior instead of from his parents
made him feel important. Another person had taken him seriously!

What we need is more of what Francis of Assisi had, as
described by G. K. Chesterton:

> St. Francis deliberately did not see the wood for the trees. It
> is even more true that he deliberately did not see the mob for the men.
> . . . He only saw the image of God multiplied but never monotonous.
> To him a man was always a man and did not disappear in a dense
> crowd any more than in a desert. . . . There was never a man who
> looked into those brown burning eyes without being certain that
> Francis Bernardone was really interested in him, in his own inner
> individual life from the cradle to the grave; that he himself was being
> valued and taken seriously.[5]

Experience verifies that when someone pays attention to us, it does
give us the feeling of being a person of worth.

*One practical way of taking others seriously is by listening
to them.* When I listen to you I am saying, "You are important!"
Failing to listen communicates the opposite. After a weekend retreat
at Kaleo Lodge, a man wrote to me the following: " . . . I stayed home
from work Monday, and after we sent our kids to school Jane and I
just talked for five hours. Really talked for the first time in nine years
of marriage. It is a weird feeling writing that statement. I've heard
other people say that so many times, but I knew that Jane and I could
always talk. I realize now that I did a lot of talking and not much
listening."

This form of neglect can occur in any of our relationships.
Perhaps the people it is easiest not to hear are our children. We
become so accustomed to providing for them that we can slip into the
role of thinking for them too. We assume that we know what they are
feeling without their telling us, because we know what we are feeling
for them. But they are not an extension of us. They too are unique,
unrepeatable miracles of God who must pursue their own destiny,
with or without our help.

This year we have entered a new era at our house: we have our first teen-ager. The changes occurring are incredible and delightful. David has just discovered that maybe girls do have a place in the scheme of things. At the same time he is beginning to assert himself in much stronger ways. He is testing his mother's authority and pushing lightly against his father's. I am certain the need to try his own wings will become much more intense as he progresses.

While I expect that I will make my share of mistakes, I am also extremely excited about this new adventure with our older son. I want to give him growing room and learn with him and from him. I want to hear him and understand him. Because I love him, I want to take him seriously, especially as he moves from being a boy to being a man. What could delight a father's heart more than seeing his son standing on his own feet as a man — a man who knows he has a place in God's world and that others do as well? I have made a commitment to him to that end, and to that end I will give him all I have under Christ to help. God grant us wisdom!

It is even harder to be a listener in our less intimate relationships. We can get so caught up in thinking that we must solve everyone else's problem that we hardly wait for the other person to finish sharing before we give an "answer" or suggest a "solution." But we need to learn as the Christian community that God became an answer for us in Christ and that He purposes to incarnate in His people that answer. All men desperately need to know that God really hears them, and one primary way God has chosen for the world to be touched by this reality is for His people to participate in His listening.

I remember several years ago when this truth came home to me dramatically as "good news." I had been invited by a friend, who was nibbling at the Christian faith, to a cocktail party at his home . Now, cocktail parties had not been a part of my normal circuit as a minister, but I wanted to go because of the friendship that had developed. I also felt at liberty to go by recalling that Christ was truly a friend to those the religious community shunned in His day. But, not being all that free in those days, I decided to lay some plans for the evening. I did not want to make anyone uncomfortable any more than I wanted to be uncomfortable. So I decided ahead of time to look around the room for the loneliest-looking person there and do what I could to make his evening less lonely.

Well, it did not take long to find that person — a man about forty who looked as though he had just lost every friend in the world, if indeed he had ever had any. I went over to him, stuck out my hand, and told him my name; he told me his and I asked, "How is it going with you?" I learned that you should not ask that kind of question unless you really want to know. Ed told me how it was going with him for the next forty-five minutes. His divorce was final, and his life was in shambles. He was really hurting, and I *listened*.

After he finished his story, Ed wanted me to wait because he noticed another person at the party he wanted me to know. He kept bringing people into our conversation, and others included their friends until we had forty people in the den sharing, laughing, and really enjoying ourselves. I was the last to leave the party and probably had as much, if not more, fun than anyone. My listening released Ed and included him in the party. He in turn included everyone he could reach in the personal interaction that transpired in my friend's den. It was refreshing to discover at that cocktail party the kind of relationship that Jesus Christ must have had!

Along with being heard, *every human being needs affirmation*. It is a tragic mistake if in my relationships with others I focus only on their problems. In so doing I communicate either verbally or nonverbally that they are "not okay" people. Most people, as it is, carry inside themselves plenty of this "not okay" material and are acting out just that. Therefore, to have your worth as a person acknowledged and affirmed is extremely important for your journey toward wholeness.

Sometimes a person may be carrying so many negative feelings about himself that he cannot respond positively to your affirmation. He may turn it off with the underlying feeling that "if you really knew about me, you wouldn't say that." Stronger measures may be needed to break through such a negative grid. But I am convinced, along with many others, that we must experience a valid "welcome to the human race" from another human being in order to feel that we belong. This is part of God's will for us — that we experience community and participate in extending that community to others!

Positive recognition of others is needed at every level of human interaction. The first few years of our marriage were difficult, because from a practical standpoint I was married to my vocation. There is a difference between being dedicated to one's task and being married to it. My ministry was extremely challenging and fulfilling, and I became so engrossed in it that I lost sight of my wife and her needs as a person. This was an immature and selfish thing to do on my part, but I did it.

One night as I was speaking on "family relations" it hit me: I was not practicing what I was teaching. It was as though someone had turned the lights on for me. The area of my blindness was suddenly set forth in bold relief. God had given me a beautiful person to love and to share life with, and I had taken her for granted and gone off to "change the world."

That night Verdell and I had a long talk. I admitted to her my mistake. Now, pure human pride keeps that from being an easy thing to do, but facing up to our errors opens the door to all kinds of creative possibilities.

I told Verdell that I loved her more than anything else in the world and that I couldn't make it without her and didn't even want to try. At that point our communication moved from the verbal level to the tears level. It was great to cry together and to affirm our love for each other after such a long drought. That experience of affirmation gave Verdell the kind of security in our relationship that she needed in order to work through some fears she had about being the wife of a minister and the mother of our first little boy.

If we consciously or unconsciously become so absorbed in either the excitement or the struggle of our own life that we lose sight of the significance of the *others* around us, the result will be destructive. In the end it will leave us *alone.*

Hopefully we will not wait for such a painful awakening before we realize that we need to affirm others and we begin to give positive recognition.

Recently I witnessed a refreshing miracle in this matter at one of our Bible studies. Before the study begins we usually spend time informally visiting with one another while waiting for late-comers. This brief fellowship period is often as significant for many people as the study itself. During this recent fellowship period Ray shared with George and me a decision he was wrestling with regarding a change of jobs. Another bank had offered him an enticing position. The struggle came at the point of leaving a very secure job of fourteen years to risk a new opportunity in a growing but smaller bank. George responded by giving Ray so much personal affirmation that Ray did not know what to do with it at first. George said, "Ray, that's fantastic, even that they would offer you that position. It shows that they really believe you are their man! Whatever you decide, I'm excited for you and will be praying for you as you struggle with the decision!"

Ray's face lit up. Here was another businessman who affirmed him and who said, "I'm for you!" Needless to say, Ray was so open and enthusiastic during the Bible study that it was a pleasure to watch him. And George was just as excited as Ray. That's what affirmation does for people — frees them to enjoy themselves and each other as nothing else will.

Mutual need-satisfaction must be a focal point for any lasting relationship. God is the only being who is complete and adequate within Himself. He needs nothing or no one except as He chooses to need us out of His love for us. All other beings, including man, are creatures of need and are pushed by those needs to find fulfillment. In fact, all of life can be viewed from a need-fulfillment perspective. Our search for God comes because there is a "God-shaped" vacuum within every human being that God alone can satisfy. Our flight from God comes as a basic expression of our rebellion, in which we must remain aloof from God to maintain our self-centered existence.

From the cradle to the grave we function out of a complex "need" system, and within our humanity there will always remain a degree of incompleteness. This sense of incompleteness is not a curse but a blessing. Because of it we struggle on, exploring the deeper meanings of our own being, of God's, and of those with whom we dwell. Marriage and the birth of children are expressions of our need for intimacy. Our work partially expresses our need for a meaningful place among men, while our effort to cultivate friendships expresses our need to belong. The positions and possessions we pursue are efforts to gain power and security.

Seeking to understand myself in the light of the biblical faith and personal reactions has opened many doors for understanding others. The good news of the Christian faith is that personal fulfillment always comes in the context of mutual fulfillment. Adequate meeting of my needs comes only as I am meeting the needs of others. We cannot live in this world alone and know any degree of completeness.

Making the "leap of faith" by receiving Jesus Christ as God's Son and our Savior allows God to become a living reality within our experience and gives us a beautiful awareness that we are no longer estranged and alone in the universe. The One who is at the core of all reality and life dwells within us, and He brings with Him possibilities beyond our wildest dreams! Still, He does not free us from our need to be meaningfully related to other persons. The opposite is true. He heightens our need for others when He brings us into His family, by giving us the assignment to "love one another as I have loved you." In fact the only objective evidence we have that we love God is our love for His people. The only way we can serve Him is by serving others.[6] So from either perspective — man without God or man with God — human beings have needs which only other human beings can satisfy. But by being open and receptive to God's love and life within, we increase enormously the potential for growth-evoking relationships.

More than one person who has lost his spouse through either death or divorce, and who has not yet been able to move beyond the loss, has told me, "I believe in God. Why doesn't He remove this loneliness?" God can help us, but He never takes someone else's place in our lives. He will not take a husband's or wife's place, a child's place, a parent's place, or anyone else's. Were He to do so, He would simply be contributing to our isolation from other people. His desire for us is community! He can help us survive, heal, and move on to invest more of ourselves in other relationships, but never does He remove the need for those relationships.

There are certain *needs* that every healthy relationship must fulfill, such as positive recognition, communication of true feelings, real caring, growth-evoking transactions of various kinds.

And there are *unique needs* that must be fulfilled within each relationship — i.e., husband/wife; parent/child; teacher/student; employer/employee — and between friends whose relationships will always be changing.

Remember that growth demands that there be a mutual need-fulfillment process occurring at all times. When the process is blocked, the relationship withers and conflict increases.

A word of caution — do not expect equal doses of *giving* and *receiving* to occur within any relationship. We are not mechanical robots swapping favors, but rather human beings who need flexibility and freedom. Today one person may be giving more and the other receiving more. But everyone has the need both to give and to receive, whether or not they recognize it. Hopefully the position of the one giving more and the one who is receiving will alternate as they respond to one another's needs.

Some practical questions one might ask himself in examining his "need fulfillment" are these: What needs do I have that are being met by this relationship? What needs am I meeting in this relationship? How fulfilling is the relationship? What can I do to make it more fulfilling?

We cannot change others. To set out on a direct course of attempting to force change will only increase the conflict. By altering our reactions and patterns of behavior we increase the possibility for others to change in response to our change. So the primary question becomes: What creative changes can I make that will meet his needs sufficiently to warrant a change in him?

Several years ago as a pastor I discovered the reality of the necessity of making changes in ourselves as the only possible way for resolving bitter conflict. I had a dream for the church I served. The dream was for that traditional congregation to become a loving, caring community which would support each of its members in the world. I was so sure that this was the New Testament pattern that I gave myself totally to the realization of that dream. A core group caught the vision and they did become a ministering community which the majority of the membership affirmed and celebrated.

But I failed to realize how threatening and revolutionary a "ministering laity" can be to the traditional, clergy-oriented concept of church life. There were some who rebelled at the idea of non-professionals speaking and taking such active roles in every area of ministry. Frankly, I was not aware, until a confrontation occurred, that this group was so uptight about the direction we were pursuing. I was at fault for being insensitive. The confrontation created a bitter conflict. I was hurt and angry, and so was everyone else. Those whose lives had been blessed as they had become involved in ministry felt strongly about moving ahead. Those who were threatened and who, because of their hesitation, had lost some of their leadership in the church felt equally positive that we needed to return to a more traditional pattern.

All our efforts at reconciliation failed. The lines were clearly drawn, and no one would move from his position. It took me some time to sort through my own feelings and to realize that the only way I could initiate a possible change was for me to change my own attitudes. I began to understand why certain individuals had been threatened by our lay-oriented approach to church life and ministry. I realized that I had failed as a pastor to be sensitive to what was developing and therefore had not been able to hear those who were negative about the situation. When I admitted in a message my failure to be sensitive and my inability to really accept weakness in myself or others, and shared the hope I had because of God's grace and forgiveness, people changed. The person who had been most vocal about our having led the church in this new direction came to me and apologized for having reacted as she had. We confessed to one another and cried together. The release that came was something wonderful.

I am not naive enough to think that everything always works out when we make the proper shifts within ourselves, because they do not. But I am certain that we create a much greater opportunity for alteration when we first become willing to change in healthy ways.

Just as there are needs that can be supplied only by other persons, there are also needs that God alone can meet. Therefore, if we try to force another human being into the role of meeting all our needs, the result will be increased conflict and real possibility of destroying the entire relationship. We must remember that every person has limitations. Demanding too much drives others from us.

God alone can give us loving attention twenty-four hours a day. And His love is not bent toward indulging or spoiling us.

Every objective we have discussed is but a facet of love, for authentic love is the most inclusive dynamic known in human interchange. The title *Love or Perish* says it concisely. Without love we all perish, and so do our relationships. Throughout life our health and our happiness depend upon our ability to love and our willingness to allow others to love us.

To love and to allow oneself to be loved is more difficult for some than for others. The more love and security we were given as children, and the more adequate our parent models were in this, the easier it will be for us to engage others from this open posture. We cannot give to another what we do not possess. Therefore it is imperative that we be on the receiving end first in order to give with any depth.

Since we did not choose our parents and cannot go back and relive any part of our lives, are we locked into determinism by what happened to us in our early years? No!

The capacity of self-direction and change that we have previously discussed means that although we have been deeply influenced by our past, we are not hopeless victims of it. We can and do seek other sources of love, and herein lies our hope. Love can come to us through a friend or a spouse — or a child, for that matter. And if we cannot find it there, it comes to us in its purest and fullest form in Jesus Christ. Most of us need another person to help make God's love real and believable. But whether we have that person or not, His love is there reaching out to us through whatever channels are available.

One man related in a weekend conference that while he was in a strange city, God's love became real to him in the midst of his desperation. He had gone to his motel room with the intention of taking his life. But he noticed the Bible which the Gideons had placed there, picked it up, and began to read. As he read, God's love engulfed him, and he began to weep and pray. It was incredible to him to think that the God who created the universe could love and accept him. He prayed, "God, if what I am reading is real, help me!"

That prayer changed his life. He felt the love and forgiveness of God as never before, and hope came which dispelled the darkness that had robbed him of his desire to live. The enthusiasm that radiated from him as he shared his story gave us the sense that God was loving us through him.

I have watched Bob McGhee, a Young Life leader in Dallas, bring scores of high-school kids to Christ by loving them. He is committed to those youth. He identifies with them by going to their games and to the places where they hang out. He engages them in conversation, listens, and responds to the needs they let him in on as best he can. After he has won the right to be heard, he shares his faith. They hear him because they know he cares about them. That is the norm for sharing one's faith effectively.

The greatest description of love in literature states that

> love is very patient and kind, never jealous or envious, never boastful or proud, never haughty or selfish or rude. Love does not demand its own way. It is not irritable or touchy. It does not hold grudges and will hardly even notice when others do it wrong. It is never glad about injustice, but rejoices whenever truth wins out. If you love someone you will be loyal to him no matter what the cost. You will always believe in him, always expect the best of him, and always stand your ground in defending him. Love never fails — never fades out or becomes obsolete.[7]

Only God can love like that! True. But as we make *love* a viable goal in our relationships, we increase the creative potential in those relationships beyond measure.

If you would entreat God for a gift, ask Him for the *gift of love*, for it is the greatest of all gifts and brings with it a quality of life that does more to bless and free people than all the other gifts combined.

Questions for Personal Reflection and Group Interaction

1. How much of your energy are you currently spending in an effort to change someone else? How is it working?
2. Do you feel pressure from others to change? How are you responding to their pressure?

3. Do you see yourself as being carried along by your circumstances, or as one swimming upstream against his circumstances?
4. What is your goal in your significant relationships?
5. When conflict arises, do you attack or withdraw? In what way?
6. Socially, into what class or category would you place yourself — upper, middle, or lower?
7. Would your classification be based more on money or education or on the crowd you run with?
8. Do you see yourself as one of the "little people" or as one of the decision-makers?
9. How do you respond to people who are considered to be "beneath you"?
10. In what way are you attempting to call forth the good in your spouse? In your boss? In your employee? In your friend?
11. Do you recognize any negative response patterns in yourself? What do you plan to do about them?
12. How do you think other people see you?
13. On a scale from 0 to 10, how would you rate yourself as a listener?
14. How do you attempt to send messages of affirmation — by saying something, by doing something, or by thinking something?
15. Which is harder, giving to or receiving from another? Why?
16. How many people would you say you are "loving" in the biblical sense at present? How many people are "loving" you?
17. How would you describe a meaningful relationship?

3. Adding Fuel to the Fire

IN EVERY SIGNIFICANT relationship, conflict inevitably occurs. The more intimate the relationship, the greater the frequency of conflict. We all have rough edges that rub others wrong occasionally. We make mistakes, take others for granted, act out varying degrees of selfishness, and have blind spots that make us hard to live with at times. Also, conflict may arise simply because people are different — different in thought, feelings, reactions, needs, and expectations. Therefore the presence of conflict does not necessarily mean that one or both are *wrong*. No one need feel guilty about every conflict that emerges.

It is important to remember that not all conflict is bad. It is simply a reality that will emerge at some point within every relationship of any duration. *The question is not whether we will have conflict, but how we will handle it when it arises*. What will be our attitude toward the other person or persons involved? Will the struggle facilitate growth, or destroy the bond we have? The choice is ours.

Most of us are probably not consciously aware of how we

react when facing personal conflict. We simply act out the patterns
we picked up from our parent-models or from a trial-and-error system
practiced over the years. But, as in every other aspect of life, the more
real *understanding* we possess about ourselves and what we are
doing, the better our chances of coping become. This is one of the
major values of seeking the counsel of a third person — someone who
can be objective enough to help us understand where we are and what
we may be doing that is blocking any resolution.

Following are some typical reactions which only serve to
make matters worse in any given conflict. They are given, not to
enable us to pass judgment on others, but rather to stimulate examination of our own reactions and to encourage creative change where
needed.

Attacking the person instead of the problem occurs with
alarming regularity when friction develops between two individuals.
And we can become very adept at this art with minimal practice.

The issue may be family finances or discipline or any one
of a multitude of personal problems. Instead of facing the issue
squarely and dealing with it, we lash out at the other's self-esteem,
and the war is on.

These are some common patterns:

(1) Name-calling — "You're stupid," or "You really think
you're the big man"

(2) Reminding the other person of every mistake he has ever
made

(3) Asserting that the only mistake you made was ever getting
involved with him in the first place

(4) Identifying them with another person as a put-down —
"You're just like your father"

(5) Taunting questions — "When are you ever going to grow
up and act like an adult?"

Cutting another person off by *refusing to talk about the situation* does
not help either. This can be done with a single statement — "I don't
want to talk about it" — or with a curse word, a glare, or silence.
What is communicated in this act is either the feeling that whatever
the problem is, it's not important enough to discuss or the feeling that

the other person is not important enough at that moment to talk with. Either way, it's a put-down that stirs vigorous hostility.

Exaggeration hampers creative interchange. By interjecting such inclusive words as "never" and "always," the problem is enlarged far beyond any particular incident that may have triggered it. "You never do anything right" or "You always make a mess" catches up every other sticky issue, real or imagined, in the relationship. And that is too much to resolve at one sitting.

Also, the problems in any painful conflict have a tendency to grow in the minds and emotions of the parties involved. We take the apparent facts and add our feelings to them, with devastating results at times. *Facts plus feelings* can equal disaster in any relationship unless the persons involved have a good degree of emotional health.

A person with little ego strength may be so threatened by a conflict that he begins to imagine that the other person is out to get him, his job, his reputation, or whatever he prizes in that situation. The man caught here reads into every word and gesture negative input from his own feelings. Until he can regain some sense of worth and security, he cannot deal with his conflict realistically.

I am reminded of a young man who came to me in utter despair. He had become attracted to two girls over the past year. Having asked each for a date and being refused, he announced to me that he was so unattractive that he probably never would be able to find a girl who would marry him. That is a typical expression of an overreaction to a mild but real form of rejection.

Self-justification gets in the way of any healthy resolution of strife. Making our irresponsible behavior a virtue instead of a vice by excuses and implications that blame belongs elsewhere diverts our attention from the real problem. This attitude can be expressed as the feeling "I am okay, but you are not; or they are not; or the situation is not." The individual assumes the posture of being the victim instead of the villain: "You did it to me" or "They did it to me" or "My circumstances did it to me."

Self-justification can also be an expression of an individual's effort to hide his own "not okay" feelings. This then becomes his attempt to survive in the situation. Have you ever pointed up another's weakness to keep your own from looking so bad?

5   *Self-pity adds fuel to the conflict for both the one expressing it and the one confronting it.* Feeling sorry for oneself really does not help in any situation. Yet it is easy to fall into that poor-me, it's-all-happening-to-me, no-one-understands, no-one-cares, I'm-not-appreciated, no-one-ever-had-it-this-bad cycle. But self-pity is like quicksand — the more we churn in it, the deeper we go and the further removed we become from any real help or healing. There is no way we can understand or empathize with another person while we are locked in our pity. Thus we are in no condition to work through even minor irritations. And the person being confronted by us in that state will probably experience anger or disgust toward us.

In summation, we could say that the more selfish our attitudes and interests are in a given relationship, the more fuel we have available for destroying one another.

God grant us the wisdom to be sensitive to others and the courage to change our own destructive reactions. amen.

Questions for Personal Reflection and Group Interaction

1. What do you do with your mistakes?
2. How did your parents handle conflict?
3. Have you been guilty of attacking the person instead of the problem in your conflict? How?
4. Do you ever use the "silent treatment"? What reasons prompted such action?
5. How do you feel when someone is giving you the "silent treatment"?
6. Are you prone to exaggerate the situation?
7. Which do you use more frequently — self-justification or self-pity?
8. What steps are you taking to allow more understanding both of yourself and of the other person?

4. Substitutes for Intimacy

EVERY HUMAN BEING has a deep need for closeness. We were made, not for isolation, but for community. And within the human community there must be one or more persons with whom we can relate intimately. Without such relationships our life remains barren and unfulfilled. To be in the company of another person who allows us the freedom to explore the vast dimensions of our own unique self, and who aids in that exploration by inviting us to be a part of his inner discoveries, is to touch the miracle of life itself.

Strangely enough, there is not only this need for closeness but also a *fear of it.* The sources of this fear are varied, but primarily it is inherent in our estrangement from God. All of life bears witness to our *dependence on something or someone* other than ourselves for our very existence. Our persistent assertion of independence — i.e., playing God for ourselves and attempting to do the same for others — leaves us with an uneasiness that cannot keep from making us afraid of closeness. Until this posture is reversed and dependence upon God is established, we do not have a secure foundation from which to move into intimacy.

Guilt is another potent source of fear. There is a story in the Old Testament that illustrates dramatically the power of guilt in producing fear. In Leviticus 26, the Lord declares that if the people obey Him and do right, they shall be able to defeat their enemies. "Five of you will chase a hundred, and a hundred of you, ten thousand! You will defeat all of your enemies. . . . I will walk among you and be your God, and you shall be my people."[1] Then the Lord declares that if they rebel against Him and go their own selfish way, a part of His judgment will be that "you will even run when no one is chasing you!"[2]

A clear conscience increases courage, but a guilt-ridden conscience multiplies fear. One fear that guilt fosters is the *fear of being found out*. How can we afford to move close to another person if we are afraid of being exposed?

True guilt can be resolved only by confessing the wrong to God and, when appropriate, to the person wronged and asking for forgiveness. Remember, confession is more than simply acknowledging the situation. It is agreeing with God concerning the wrong and being willing to be cured so as not to repeat the same mistake. Then we must take the second step and forgive ourselves. This opens the way for intimate relationships to flourish.

The third origin for *fear of closeness* is the rejection we have experienced. At home and among peers, rejection always comes as a devastating blow. To have parents who were able to communicate acceptance and love is a tremendous asset and preparation for our journey through life. Teachers and friends who gave us that same sense of *safeness*, and who dealt with our mistakes realistically without communicating rejection, blessed us far beyond our awareness. But if we failed to have predominantly positive relationships in our childhood, or if we have come through a crushing experience of rejection such as divorce, being fired, or losing a close friend, we may legitimately be wary of being hurt again. If this be the case, we need to acknowledge our fear, give ourselves some time to recover partially, and then force ourselves, if necessary, to take definite steps toward a depth involvement with some of the significant people in our lives.

If we fail to resolve our fear of intimacy, we may seek substitutes for it. Intimacy and love are so intertwined and essential to life that they cannot be separated or substituted. Therefore any attempt to replace them will be damaging to the person and his relationships.

It is not uncommon to find that we may be substituting power for intimacy. This struggle emerges most easily in the family or in organizational structure ranging from a business operation to a social club. Whenever there is opportunity to gain control over another person at any level, there will be the temptation to opt for power rather than intimacy.

Child abuse is an extreme expression of this malady. The parent is bigger and feels that he has the right to make the child do his wishes by whatever amount of force he chooses to exert.

A husband may become extremely domineering as a result of his fear of intimacy. By controlling totally his wife's movements and thoughts he thinks he may achieve the closeness for which he longs.

A boss in a company may substitute ironclad control to avoid human contact with his employees. He may honestly believe that if he can manage his people without personal involvement, he will achieve more. But is any achievement worth the loneliness that comes from working beside people for years without ever being touched by them? What are a man's real achievements anyway — reaching a materialistic goal? Exerting power over others? Living life to its fullest? Of course, each must answer that question for himself, but regardless of how he answers, the need for closeness remains.

Attempting to possess another person is a poor substitute for closeness. This is our temptation to treat another as though he belonged to us, like part of our property. In this we reduce him in our thinking to an object of ownership rather than a unique human being with infinite potential. This may influence his self-image to such a degree that he sees himself as a person of little worth. Or he may resent us and pull away as fast as he can. He may even retaliate out of deep bitterness.

Making possessions of people can happen in any relationship, but it occurs most often between parents and their offspring. We can relate to our children as though they are simply extensions of ourselves, completely overlooking the fact that they have minds and personalities exclusively their own.

Recently I counseled a man who presented as his problem a deep sense of despair. As he shared his situation, it became obvious that for years he had been building up hostility against his father. The father had always created a place for the son, a place where the father could continue to make the real decisions. The son had never been listened to or taken seriously as a person. He was ready to explode, yet he could not understand why he felt as he did. He had accepted his father's image of him and was faithfully living it out, but within him a war was raging. He needed to break free and be his own man, but how could he go against the dreams of a father who "loved" him so much?

When I suggested that he talk with his father about his feelings and his need to do something on his own, he said, "I couldn't do that. We're not that close!" No, they were not that close. The father had substituted total possession of his son for intimacy. He had never asked his son for any of his ideas or about any of his feelings, but had assumed that he knew the son and knew what was best for him.

One of the greatest gifts we can give our children is accepting their uniqueness and joining with them to release their creativity and potential.

Manipulation is a deadly substitute for intimacy. We are defining *manipulation* as an interpersonal transaction in which one or both persons involved has an ulterior motive. Eric Berne identifies this procedure as "game playing": "It is socially programed in the sense that it follows an automatic, predictable sequence. It is when relationships become non-manipulative, when they lose their hidden motivations, and become individually programed, that is, spontaneous and expressive of the person, that intimacy begins."[3]

Christ confronted the religious leaders of His day with the pretense inherent in their games. He said of them, "For they don't do what they tell you to do. They load you with impossible demands that they themselves don't even try to keep. Everything they do is for show."[4] Jesus knew that manipulation always leads to exploitation.

Putting a "snow job" on anyone for any reason prevents an authentic interchange from occurring. *Honesty* and *sincerity* are essential for enduring relationships. When the disciples were arguing over which of them would be greatest in the kingdom, "Jesus called a small child over to him and set the little fellow down among them, and said, 'Unless you turn to God from your sins and become as little children, you will never get into the Kingdom of Heaven.' "[5] The little child represented humility, openness, and spontaneity. Children have a way of coming at things head-on. If they want to know about something, they ask. There is enough candor in them that it is easy to see what they are thinking and why, if we but pay attention. Children are excellent models for the kind of honesty we need within every significant relationship.

Oversocializing is a deterrent to intimacy and is characterized by superficial contacts with an impressive number of casual acquaintances. Attempting to know everyone can end in not knowing anyone, really. Love and intimacy require time and nurture to grow. Therefore we cannot build depth relationships with a large number of people at one time. But the more depth we experience with a few people, the better equipped we will be for relating meaningfully to that larger segment of acquaintances.

A friend who is taking his commitment to Christ very seriously shared in one of our groups that his circle of friends had narrowed since becoming a Christian. Previously he tried to establish casual acquaintances with as many people as possible. But he admitted that he really did not have any close friends. Now he and his wife are learning to walk with a few couples who are giving themselves intensely to following Christ. Real friendships have developed and, with the support of this smaller community, they are becoming increasingly effective in touching the larger community meaningfully.

Christ gave us the model when He poured Himself primarily into twelve men. Instead of trying to touch everyone lightly, He touched a few men deeply enough to change the course of history and the destiny, not only of those twelve men, but also of the many who have followed.

Do you have one other person or, better yet, a support group with whom you are building deep relationships? If not, ask the Lord to help you find or start such a group. Look for people who are hurting or who at least are seeking more than they have found. Discontent can be fertile ground for new life.

Questions for Personal Reflection
and Group Interaction

1. Do you recognize both the "need for closeness" and the "fear of closeness" in your own life? Why do you fear it, if you do?
2. How many people would you say you are really close to?
3. Do you think these same people feel close to you?
4. How do you handle your guilt?
5. In what experience have you felt great rejection?
6. How did you respond to that experience of rejection?
7. Are you possessive? Have you ever been accused of being possessive?
8. Are you domineering? Have you ever been accused of being domineering?
9. How do you respond to being manipulated?
10. Do you prefer to spend more time alone, or more time with others?
11. On a scale from 0 to 10, how would you score yourself on contentment?
12. What substitutes have you used for intimacy?
13. In what experience or relationship have you felt the most acceptance?

5. Managing Your Emotions

CONFLICT TRIGGERS strong emotions within all of us. But because we all possess a unique history and have our own peculiar sensitivities and response patterns, we do not necessarily feel the same things when confronted with conflict. To assume that others feel the same way we do, or to insist that their emotional make-up be a duplicate of our own, can be a fatal mistake — the deathblow to the development of a deep relationship.

A man I knew had the best intentions, but because he could not give others permission to feel things differently than he, he always suppressed any risk-sharing in the small groups he led. Though he was totally unaware of the detrimental effect he had, people who were shaky about their own identity or direction were afraid to share their uncertain and sometimes negative feelings in his presence. What he communicated was *conditional acceptance*. His acceptance was extended only to those who, from his aggressive perspective, were committing their lives to Christ. The person struggling to find who he was or what he had to commit felt terribly uncomfortable and could not share his true feelings in that setting. The leader felt good about the positive responses gained from the group, but some of the participants went away feeling rejected or guilty for not having it all together. Interaction that was designed to facilitate discovery and growth actually blocked both, and the intended blessing turned out to be a kind of curse. The participants felt judged and condemned instead of understood and loved.

A judgmental attitude produces despair, while understanding creates hope. It is hard for us to remember, unless we keep our own needs in focus, that the innermost depths of the human heart are revealed only to love. This is the reason why the people Christ met felt free to share their true feelings and to ask their real questions. His mission was not one of condemnation, but one of promise!

The first step in giving acceptable expression to our emotions is willingness to become aware of what we are feeling and why we are feeling it. In writing this chapter I have discovered the *why* of some feelings I have been struggling with for several years. I came to Dallas a decade ago with a vision — a vision to build a Christian community that would release the gifts and potential of its members for ministry in and to the world. At the same time this group would become an authentic model for the larger circle of believers who wanted to be a complementary part of the body of Christ in the real world.

I was not interested in the monastic or communal approach to community. I did not want to pull people out of the world, but to create a community in the thick of daily life that would serve as leaven to the whole human enterprise. For this reason I have spent a great deal of time in the business arena of this city. Where people live is where the liberating power of Christ and His people must be felt. And it must be felt in word and deed! To talk about the love of Christ without embodying love or integrity negates the message. Not that we can ever say it or be it or do it perfectly, but to be authentic in our walk with Christ and our concern for others does make the gospel message believable. In humility, recognizing our faults and shortcomings, we can share our hope with that part of the world we touch.

The focus of my emotional struggle was my increasing resistance to broadcasting this vision to the world. Friends who became involved in our ministry kept insisting that we sell Christian

Concern far and wide. I had strong feelings against this approach, but could not understand why. I felt sure that the reason had to be more than my natural inclination to resist the role of "religious promoter." I wanted to share the vision but not to promote joining Christian Concern as the primary means for experiencing community. Slowly I discovered that my ambivalent feelings were coming from changes occurring within me. This awareness and acceptance of my feelings lessened my turmoil.

Being relieved of the pressure to create, promote, or sustain a community myself was freeing indeed. My vision remained, but my approach changed.

I am not trying so hard as I was to *make community happen*. Rather I am attempting to *let it happen* and to be a participant and an observer of it instead of its creator. I have discovered that God must get distressed with visionary dreamers: our dreams can make us proud and pretentious.

> The man who fashions a visionary ideal of community demands that it be realized by God, by others, and by himself. He enters the community of Christians with his demands, sets up his own law, and judges the brethren and God Himself accordingly. He stands adamant, a living reproach to all others in the circle of brethren. He acts as if he is the creator of the Christian community, as if his dream binds men together. When things do not go his way, he calls the effort a failure. When his ideal picture is destroyed, he sees the community going to smash. So he becomes, first an accuser of his brethren, then an accuser of God, and finally the dispairing accuser of himself.[1]

God creates community. He alone has the power to bind men together. And He alone can judge the success or the failure of any venture. It is precisely this conviction that gives me a terribly uneasy feeling when I am called upon to speak about the "great things God is doing" through the Christian Concern Foundation fellowship. Christian Concern has been the most exciting, creative, and seemingly productive venture of my life and ministry. Yet I can only bear witness to the way God has touched me and others who have shared with me through this ministry. It is a success in my eyes, but that is a selfish and subjective evaluation. Each person who has participated in this fellowship will have to make his or her own evaluation, though final appraisal must lie with God alone.

Coming to the above perspective has been one of the most liberating experiences of my life. It makes each of us responsible for our obedience to Christ, but not responsible for the outcome of a ministry that is bigger than all of us put together. We need a vision from God for our ministry, but we must guard against that vision's becoming our god.

The men who were instrumental in beginning this experimental ministry agreed that the mission was to share the good news of Christ and not the good news of a foundation. Those men and others who came after them have remained true to that commitment.

The next time you find yourself caught in or moving toward a conflict, ask yourself, *What am I feeling?* When you have come through the experience, reflect on the different emotions that surfaced and ask yourself, *Why did I feel the way I did? What triggered this emotion and that emotion?* This will help you get in touch with your feelings and may enable you to discover the *why* of your response pattern.

Another good exercise to help you become aware of the emotions within is to take thirty minutes or so at the end of a day and recall the people and events you experienced that day. Try to focus on the way you felt in different situations with different people. See if you can discover *why* you reacted as you did. Insights may come slowly, but they will come as you sensitize yourself to the inner workings of the world of your own feelings.

Our response patterns emanate from both our temperaments and our conditioning. The way our parent models handled conflict and the way they handled us will shape our responses more than anything else. If they were disposed to fits of anger and permitted us to act out our anger similarly, we can expect an almost irresistible drive to continue acting out our anger that way. If they suppressed their anger and vented it by other means, then we can expect to feel the same inclination.

I need to remember that I bring my whole self to everything I experience, including conflict. Therefore it is important that I become aware of what is transpiring in me in order to begin managing my emotions creatively. What is the emotion that I need to control? Why do I have such a strong urge to react in this particular manner?

Once I recognize the pattern and know what I am up against, I can start working on deliberate steps for altering the unhealthy reactions that have developed.

The two emotions that surface most often in a conflict are anger and hurt. We may become angry because we feel threatened or because we feel that the other person is trying to take advantage of us, dominate us, or blame us, or for any of a dozen other reasons. We may express our hostility by exploding and telling the other person off, by withdrawing to avoid the possibility of a blowup, or by a combination of these or other responses.

We may be hurt because we feel unloved and unaffirmed; the issues raised by the other person implicitly question either our knowledge, our actions, or our motives. A person with low self-esteem tends to experience hurt feelings when confronted. But a person who has an exaggerated sense of his importance may really be incensed by the audacity of anyone who disagrees with him. Anger and hurt can be devastating if they are not dealt with properly. To deny the presence of either emotion when indeed one does exist causes the conflict to move underground. Clinebell aptly states that such action is like storing dynamite in the basement of one's home. On the other hand, to allow uncontrolled irruption of these emotions alienates everyone involved.[2]

We must decide between two commitments before we have any hope of changing these strong emotional upsets. *Am I committed to always winning in the conflict?* Or, *am I committed to being meaningfully related to my spouse, boss, friend, or any person with whom I am experiencing difficulties?* Some of us are so committed to being right that the other person does not have a chance to fight with us creatively. This posture is destructive to everyone involved. And the call of Christ confronts us at this point with great force. Christ said, "This is my commandment, That you love one another as I have loved you."[3] To be committed to Christ is to be committed to His people. This does not mean that we shall never get angry. Quite the opposite: the person who cannot feel anger cannot feel love. Christ expressed anger to the Pharisees,[4] to Peter,[5] to the moneychangers in the temple who were exploiting the people,[6] and to those who mistreated little children.[7]

Anger can be a positive force or a destructive one. Our concern here is that we take seriously our commitment of learning how to care genuinely for others and seek to express our anger in a positive manner. Expressing anger can clear the air; it can help keep a relationship honest by refusing manipulation or being taken advantage of or of being treated as less than a person. There is nothing wrong with saying, "I feel that you are not taking me seriously." Or, "I feel that you are not shooting straight with me." In so doing, you are expressing a feeling that may or may not reflect accurately the true state of affairs. But your feeling is out in the open, and the two of you can examine the situation together. At least there are some creative possibilities in an honest session, whereas to keep your mouth closed and stew about it creates headaches, ulcers, and a critical spirit.

We may be so afraid of conflict that we avoid it at all costs. We may need acceptance so badly that we cannot afford to risk rejection with any kind of disagreement. If that be the case, then we have discovered a matter that needs healing desperately. *As our security base becomes more firm, we will become less afraid of possible conflict.* Ask the living Christ to give you a deep sense of His acceptance, and keep on asking until it comes. At the same time, deliberately take some small steps toward risking more of yourself with a person or persons who you are reasonably sure care for you. No human being can give us unconditional love and acceptance all the time, but they can some of the time. Any degree of acceptance enables us to open up more completely to Christ, who does give us this perfect quality of love consistently.

Sometimes our emotions may be so out of our control that we need help in understanding and dealing with them. To recognize this and do something about it is a mark of personal strength, not weakness. We can thank God that there are people in the helping professions who can serve us well in this respect. And I might add that it is no more foolish for a Christian to go to a counselor for assistance than to a dentist for a toothache or to a doctor for an illness. Sometimes we get trapped on a negative treadmill and need God's help through one of His servants in order to break loose and breathe again the fresh air of creative response.

My wife has helped me numberless times to break out of

one of my negative response patterns. And I am deeply grateful for a longtime friend who hears most of my joys and pains and allows me to struggle and grow. We have served each other in this respect and have become as brothers. Sometimes a sensitive, caring friend may be able to give us all the help we need. At other times we may need a pro. Being willing to seek adequate help is a sign of good judgment and not of weakness. A rule of thumb: If we cannot understand what is happening within, and the significant people in our lives are not able to help us pull out of our predicament, then by all means we should look for someone with the credentials and reputation for helping people. Many times the spouse or friend may be too battered down to help. I am convinced many marriages could have been saved if professional help had been sought earlier.

There are several important steps to consider when you are confronted with a conflict.

1. Ask yourself if the anger or other negative message you are receiving belongs to you or to someone else. The way we interpret an experience determines our reaction to it. If your husband comes home and yells at you and if you receive his yelling as unjustified anger toward you, there is no way you can keep from resenting such treatment. But if you knew that the boss had been yelling at him that day, as were two or three customers, and you recognized that his yell belonged to them and not you, it would doubtless be easier to keep your cool and not take his reaction as a personal affront.

You ask, "How can I know to whom his anger belongs?" Well, you might inquire before you go to war. The husband or wife could ask the one who is coming on negatively, "Is there something we need to talk about?" or another acceptable question that would invite communication. This will give the other an opportunity to focus their anger on the thing that has upset them and not on the one they love and need desperately at that moment.

It is really amazing how many bad scenes can be avoided by calmly taking the time to find out what is going on with the other person. You may find that there is no reason for you to become defensive or hostile. My wife has abated my feelings more than once this way, and we have been able to laugh about it instead of fighting over it. It makes for pleasant togetherness instead of a hassle.

The key is to use your mind before you start your mouth.

2. Examine yourself to see if the problem lies within you. We all have the tendency to assume certain things about others and then expect them to live up to our assumptions. We draw mental pictures of what we want or need others to be and usually insist that they conform to our expectations. The problem arises when we make the other person responsible for the fallacies which are in us. We must not make the other person a prisoner of our expectations. Rather we must remain open to his self-revelation so we can develop a relationship with the real person and not with an image in our minds. Even if we once had an accurate picture of a person, we must leave him free to change, which is the nature of life itself. A brief glance through a family photograph album convinces us of the reality of physical change, although each snapshot was representative at the time. We must learn to accept the changes in every aspect of another person's life as readily as we accept the physical.

A good friend of mine became a Christian four years ago. He was a raw recruit for God's army, and a delight to the entire Christian community in this city. People were amazed at the changes in him and celebrated God's grace in his life. He knew nothing of the faith and eagerly sought understanding from friends and teachers. Because he has never done anything half-heartedly, he has been so intent on learning about the Christian faith that he is now attending a seminary part-time. His knowledge and zeal surpass that of many of his friends who were at one time his teachers. And it has not been easy for some to let him go. But let him go we must, and each other as well!

I have returned occasionally to visit the people in my two pastorates. One pastorate is sixteen years removed, and the other ten. We tended to continue to relate to each other as we had in the past. But in so many ways I am not the man I was in either pastorate, and I intuitively sense that they have changed too. Letting go can be painful, but in the end it will be infinitely more exciting and creative.

Some questions to ask are these: "Am I upset because this person has failed to be what I wanted him to be or expected him to be?" "Do I have idealistic models of father-mother, son-daughter, wife-husband, sister-brother, employer-employee, teacher-pupil, that I impose upon the real people in my life who fulfill these roles?" "Am I willing to experience the other person rather than my expectations?" "Am I freeing this person to be himself, or demanding that he act out my caricature of him?" Coming to terms with the difference between the person and our expectation is needed in every relationship and is especially pertinent in adjusting to your mate in marriage.

Another facet of our expectation syndrome is *the desire to make the other person over in our image.* The Christian community has as great a problem with this as does the world. Whatever kind of Christian we think we are or are aspiring to be, we are tempted sorely to insist that every other believer be or aspire to be the same. Instead of giving Christ the freedom to work in the other person's life at that person's pace to bring out his uniqueness and to be conformed to Christ's image, we tend to demand conformity to our system and think of ourselves as the model for that conformation. But Christ alone can furnish an adequate model for the uniqueness that is in each person.

We make a grave mistake when we attempt to remodel the personality of another or allow ourselves to be completely molded by any religious, psychological, or social system. God created us originals, and He purposes to bless and enrich others by the development of our gifts and opportunities.

Therefore, to be genuinely in touch with another person is to recognize, respect, and affirm his difference. To relate to him meaningfully demands that neither of us disappear but that we each contribute to the full realization of the other's personality. It is this kind of relationship that becomes a gift and helps us to understand better the way Christ relates to us.

3. Refuse to let yourself get locked into a critical attitude. The other person may not be meeting our expectations or our needs, and out of our frustration we can become critical. Once we surrender to a critical spirit we can no longer deal with our lives or our emotions realistically. Neither can we see the other person clearly. Critical attitudes poison relationships and leave us estranged from everyone, including ourselves. Christ said, "Judge not, that you be not judged. For with the judgment you pronounce you will be judged, and the

measure you give will be the measure you get. Why do you see the speck that is in your brother's eye, but do not notice the log that is in your own eye? Or how can you say to your brother, 'Let me take the speck out of your eye,' when there is the log in your own eye? You hypocrite, first take the log out of your own eye, and then you will see clearly to take the speck out of your brother's eye."[8] We get what we give.

If we could but understand the other person without demanding perfection, we would have less reason for being so critical of him. Karl Menninger tells a story which may focus the issue for us.

When a trout rising to a fly gets hooked on a line and finds himself unable to swim about freely, he begins with a fight which results in struggles and splashes and sometimes an escape. Often, of course, the situation is too tough for him.

In the same way the human being struggles with his environment and with the hooks that catch him. Sometimes he masters his difficulties; sometimes they are too much for him. His struggles are all that the world sees and it naturally misunderstands them. It is hard for a free fish to understand what is happening to a hooked one.[9]

Understanding will not enable us to find good people because we all share the common malady of selfishness and sin. It can, however, open to us the door of empathy rather than judgment. Without empathy for the fish that's hooked there will never be any understanding or possibility of resolving our conflicts. Who knows but that we too are hooked in ways we do not yet recognize?

4. Don't blame yourself unjustly for the failures that will inevitably come. If you find that you are the cause of conflict in a relationship, there are some steps to take: examine your actions and attitude; ask the Lord for insight; seek a Christian brother's advice; admit to the offended person where you have been wrong. If, however, the offended party refuses to allow the relationship to heal after you have done everything you know to do in good conscience, accept the conflict as his problem and move on without carrying unwarranted guilt for the failure. To move on does not necessarily mean physically, but it does mean emotionally. Sometimes the other person is not ready to resolve the difficulty, and you may have to give him emotional room and time. In that case, pour your energies and

efforts into other directions and refuse to continue the hassle.

The areas we have explored in this chapter are intended to be *way-pointers* and not an exhaustive examination of emotions and their management. Volumes have been written and are still being written on this subject. But sometimes we try to grab hold of too many ideas at once and fail to execute any of them effectively.

I have attempted to point out a few handles for changing negative reactions. Try them and then move on to others.

Questions for Personal Reflection and Group Interaction

1. Have you ever had an experience which made you acutely aware that not everyone feels the same way you do about things?
2. How easy is it for you to accept others who differ with you?
3. Would others find you hard or easy to confide in?
4. Do you have a dream or an objective that you really want to accomplish?
5. Do you have a master sentiment — one thing from which your whole life takes its meaning?
6. What do you do with your anger?
7. Are you committed to always winning in a conflict?
8. Are you afraid of conflict? How do you try to avoid it?
9. Do you feel the need to make others over in your image?
10. How do you manage your emotions?

6. Keeping the Lines of Communication Open

COMMUNICATION IS the word that best describes the moment when two people touch each other with real understanding. Despite the enormous volume of signals, verbal and nonverbal, that we send and receive within every significant relationship, only a small percentage of the *meanings* ever connect.

The reason for poor communication is that we *code* our messages and filter the others' messages through the needs, preoccupations, and prejudices of the moment. To compound the problem, we assume that we are being understood and that we understand. Without a conscious effort to decode our own messages and to recognize through which particular filter we are screening the messages given us, communication probably will not improve in our relationships. There are two words for this process: *leveling* and *listening*. Leveling is not easy; listening is even harder!

A couple of experiences from a family in our fellowship illustrate the point very well, and with some humor. Charlie is an architect and a graduate of Texas A & M. We give him fits about being an "Aggie," but he is a good sport and too sharp ever to let any of us get ahead of him. Myrna is an open person eager to learn and to discover new dimensions of life.

Charlie was in one of our early morning share groups in which one man related his experience of going to a psychologist for help in losing weight. The conclusion that he came to through the counseling was that it was all up to him. Well, Charlie, being a sharp "Aggie," decided to cut out the middleman. He took a three-by-five card and drew a picture of himself wearing polka dot shorts and standing on a scale. In the drawing he really dramatized his weight problem. At the bottom of his self-portrait he printed the words IT'S ALL UP TO YOU! Then, when he went into a restaurant to eat, he would pull out this card and lay it beside the menu to bolster his will power.

Charlie was so excited about this little device that he rushed home and showed it to his wife. Myrna took the card and looked at it a minute. Then she said, "But, Charlie, you don't have any polka dot shorts!"

They shared another experience of miscommunication that carries a lot of truth for all of us. Early one morning Myrna was downstairs having a cup of coffee when Charlie came down the stairs not feeling too well. He said, "Myrna, this morning I am just 170 pounds of anxiety, frustration, and despair." Myrna replied, "But, Charlie, you weigh more than 170 pounds!"

I cringe to think how many times I have missed the message Verdell or one of our children was sending me. Every message pointed in my direction has to come through my filter, which may be clogged up with other concern, pressures, or exhaustion. Therefore, I have to decide that I want to understand what is happening to the people around me and deliberately tune in to get their messages. Casual listening will not do.

If we keep too much of our inner space to ourselves, walls form which can lead to loneliness and even emotional divorce.

Since communication can run aground even in the best of times, how much more it gets blocked in the face of a personal conflict. One therapist says there are four common patterns of communication that occur when an individual is reacting to stress or conflict.[1] The first pattern is *placating* — always trying to please, never disagreeing, doing all in one's power to keep the other person from getting angry or rejecting him.

The second pattern is *blaming* — it's always the other person's fault. The blamer acts superior in order to get others to think he is strong.

The third pattern is *computing* — taking a head trip; acting punctiliously and reasonably; showing no emotion whatever and trying to impress others with intelligence.

The fourth pattern is *distracting* — moving off in an unrelated direction, never dealing with the issue that threatens.

Any of these four patterns may come into play when a person feels the threat of rejection or attempts to cover up anything he considers a "weakness." They are also ways to avoid being touched by another person or transparent with them. We might point out here that calling attention to someone's communication-dodge is not necessarily beneficial. If we give the other person the feeling that we are not listening, but rather labeling his conversation, then the entire communicative effort is thwarted.

A person must have genuine self-acceptance before he really has enough security to level with others. I am convinced that one of the major gifts Christ came to impart is a deep sense of acceptance. In Christ, God accepts us and frees us to accept ourselves and others!

What do we mean by *leveling?* We do not mean blowing out your feelings in such a way as to push the other person to a lower position. Rather, *it is letting your message have a single meaning and making sure it represents the truth about yourself at that moment.* "The leveling response is actually a way of responding to real people in real life situations that permit you to agree because you really do, not because you think you should; disagree because you really do, not because you think you won't make points unless you do; use your brain freely, but not at the expense of the rest of you; to change courses, not to get you off the hook, but because you want to and there is a need to do so."[2]

Practice sending clear and simple messages that represent where you are at that moment. I will send you one that will disclose my present feelings:

> I want you to read this book and enjoy it. I am excited about it and want you to be excited about it, too. But I am a little uneasy about your response. What if I write this and no one reads it? Or what if you read it and are not moved by it? I feel *vulnerable* in putting it before you for your evaluation. Yet I want to do it and am doing it! You are free to share it with your friends or burn it. I want to give you that freedom. And the only way I can is to turn it loose, and you too.

Three messages are being sent in these statements: (1) excitement, (2) anxiety, and (3) a desire to be free by giving you freedom.

Examine some of the messages you sent today. What were the main meanings? How well do you think you sent them? Did the other persons respond as if they really understood? You might ask them, if you have the opportunity, what they heard you say. Deliberately checking your signals can make you sensitive to the process, thereby increasing the possibilities for improved communication.

You can do the same with the messages being sent to you. What are you hearing the other person say? Are his gestures, facial expressions, and tone of voice sending you one message while his words transmit another? If they are, then you are receiving a message with a double meaning and you need to find out which meaning he really wants to send. When in doubt, ask the person in a spirit of acceptance to explain what he means in order to help you get the picture more accurately. Usually, if we indicate a genuine interest and concern, the individual sending the message will gladly try to clarify it to make himself understood. Experiment with this process of *decoding* and *filtering* messages. It will help you to communicate more effectively.

There are some common mistakes that usually stop the process of communication immediately.

Sharing our feelings or convictions in a way that sounds judgmental to the other person or his feelings blocks the flow of genuine communication. A young minister asked a businessman what gave his life purpose. Now, that is a heavy question which can be answered glibly or vulnerably. The businessman laid it on the line for the young minister: being able to do a good job in his vocation and thereby achieve a sense of personal satisfaction, as well as recognition from his peers that he is a worthy participant and contributor in the community. The young minister responded, "But there's no real meaning in that. What will become of your purpose when you die?"

His response may have come out of real concern, but it did not have the sound of concern in it. Rather it sounded like a "put-down." The businessman heard him saying, "You are stupid, short-sighted, and not very capable of finding an adequate purpose for your own life."

The minister failed to realize that each man has the right and the responsibility to determine the meaning for his own existence. No man can decide for another the things which will give purpose and significance to him. We each must bear witness to the meaning we have found or, in the case of the Christian, which has found us; but the autonomy and freedom that is ours as human beings insulates us against being roped into another man's system of meaning without our consent. For this reason the Christian should rejoice when another person is honest enough to reveal the *personal truth* by which he attempts to make sense out of his experience. This is a revelation of a person's inner self and should always be received as a gift. Once it is received as a gift, we can then bear witness to the meaning we have found in Christ without sounding critical. After all, it is Christ that we want people to deal with and not our criticism. And the more our witness sounds like *a gift of great value* freely shared with no intention of forcing change on the other person, the greater will be his opportunity to examine the faith for what it is.

Husband/wife roles are one place where we can easily block real interchange by an unconscious judgment. Certainly, when the husband or the wife sets out to put the other down, the flow of dialogue stops. But too often we stop it without intending to or realizing that we have. As an example, when the husband tells his wife that she is supposed to do what he wants her to do because God's plan is for her to submit, he makes her struggle at that point to be not only against the husband but also against God. That statement comes across as a double whammy, and she will either give in out of fear or get furious.

The truth of the matter is that the wife is built by God to *respond* to her husband, and the husband has the challenge of furnishing the kind of security and leadership that enables his wife to respond positively. Therefore the husband's energy needs to be directed toward caring for his wife as for his own body instead of demanding action from her on the basis of a legalistic twist of the Scripture. Together, husband and wife might go through Ephesians 5:17-33 with each focusing on his or her own role, and not on the other's. The model for the wife's response is that of the church toward Christ, and the husband's model is Christ's love for His church. What kind of head would Christ make — dogmatic and hard, or tender and strong? What would Christ furnish for her response? How does Christ long for His church to respond to Him — reluctantly and mechanically, or enthusiastically and respectfully?

We need to learn the basic principles that God has given us in the Scriptures for the family roles. But we make a terrible mistake and destroy communication if we use those principles as clubs to force the other person to conform. The question is, *How would love use these principles?* It makes better sense to concentrate on learning how, under Christ, to function in our own role. Thus we create a better opportunity for the spouse to work on his or her role with a sense of acceptance, security, and freedom.

The next time you are engaged in a conflict, instead of focusing on your own ideas and complaints, try to become aware of the feeling messages you are sending to the other person. Are you conveying judgment by your statements and emotions? Is it a put-down, or are you giving the other person the right to express himself genuinely? Once again, we come back to the real issue: *do you really want to understand and to be understood by others?* If not, it's certain you will not. But if you do, these suggestions can help you begin. Experiment with them and see what a big difference a little effort can make.

Questions for Personal Reflection
and Group Interaction

1. How would you describe real communication?
2. Are you currently aware of what is happening in the life of each member of your family? Can you identify the "growing edge" of each member of your family?
3. Do you sense that your family members are aware of what is transpiring in your life?
4. Do you see yourself as a very private person, or as a very open one?
5. Do you recognize any of the following patterns of communication operating in your life at present: *placating? blaming? computing? distracting?*
6. On a scale from 0 to 10, which number would be most representative of your degree of self-acceptance?
7. How do you level with others?
8. When you are sharing your feelings or convictions with someone else, does it ever sound as if you are pronouncing judgment upon them if they do not feel or think as you do?
9. Do you really want to understand and be understood?
10. Practice sending a single message to another person and decode it for them in the process.

7. Your Sense of Humor — A Valuable Asset

CONFLICT IS SERIOUS business! It is so serious that we cannot afford to engage in it without humor.

Real humor has its origin in the character of God, and God has endowed man with it in abundance. Who can watch the creatures of God play without smiling or even laughing? I have jokingly shared with our people that much insight into human nature has come to me in observing the animals on our ranch — whether cattle, deer, or wild turkey.

Some good examples come from our bull, named "Gus" by our kids. We got Gus when he was young and have watched him mature. One afternoon when David, our thirteen-year-old son, and I were working the cattle, we encountered a new attitude in Gus. After moving the cattle from one pen into another, I told David to run and close the gate. Gus noticed him when he started running. Evidently he thought that he had frightened David, because he shook his head and ran after him. David saw him coming and climbed the fence. Gus knew then that he had at least one person who was afraid of him.

The rest of the day he bellowed and pawed the ground every time he saw David. He obviously was proud of himself.

Gus reinforced his respect for himself over the next few weeks by chasing Verdell and my mother. His bravery was really growing! Then he took me on one morning when I was pouring out feed for the herd. He threw dirt up on his back, bellowed, and started toward me. Instead of running, I took my hat off, walked toward him, and hit him on the head with the hat. You have never seen a bull so scared! He whirled and ran as though I had hit him with a baseball bat. I called his bluff, and to this day he has never tried to chase anyone again.

Human nature is a lot like that. We try in many different ways to bluff other people, so we can keep them moving in the direction of our choosing. But inevitably the other person will one day call our bluff, and the conflict is on. Have you ever had your bluff called, or faced a situation in which the other person refused to respond to the subtle — or sometimes not so subtle — pressures you were exerting upon him? Well, it can be a very unsettling experience, but it also carries with it the potential for moving into a more honest relationship.

Recognizing the comedy inherent within our own humanity can be a real asset in resolving conflict. Seeing the difference between what we are and what we ought to be helps temper the feeling that "when our ideas conflict, I am always right." That insidious desire to make the whole world revolve around our minute knowledge and experience is in reality a tragic comedy. It becomes obvious to any thinking person that for the creature to attempt to dethrone the Creator is so ridiculous that we ought to weep over its tragedy and laugh at its absurdity. Such recognition should lead us to repentance, which is the first step toward faith in Jesus Christ.

The awareness of our own inconsistencies coupled with the promised wholeness from Christ can free us from our defensiveness and allow us to work through our conflicts with genuine concern and wholesome humor.

More than one impasse has been resolved in our marriage through the healing power of humor. Once I can laugh at myself and acknowledge my stubbornness, or whatever, to my wife, my anger dissolves. Then I am ready to deal with the issues at hand in a more reasonable vein. Besides opening the way for a more reasonable approach, humor brings the element of fun back into the relationship, which makes the conflict a stimulus for growth rather than a detriment to health.

Humor facilitates dialogue beautifully. Encountering people who hold different views politically, economically, religiously, and socially from ours is not only unavoidable, but potentially enriching. In confronting differences we may be tempted to press our point of view dogmatically. Being opinionated not only fails to win converts to our way of thinking, but also alienates the persons involved. It is a paradox that the more certain we are of the validity of our convictions, the more open we can be to those who disagree with us. The less certain we are, the stronger the need to make others conform to our view. The questions must be asked, "Do I want to express my convictions just to get them off my chest?" or "Do I believe in my convictions deeply enough to want to help the other person see their value?" The answer will reveal whether we are interested in dialogue or simply in voicing our anxiety. There seems to me to be little value in winning arguments at the expense of losing people. *amen*

If we decide that we really want to participate in the miracle of dialogue, then maintaining a good sense of humor becomes indispensable. We can become so intense and serious that we threaten the other person and block the interchange.

Recently I participated in a creative dialogue with a friend who took issue with one of my theological convictions. The exchange of ideas was stimulating, and the presence of humor kept us open. As it turned out, we were not in different theological camps at all, but were expressing our understanding of a basic biblical truth with a slightly different emphasis and application. The issue was God's sovereignty and man's freedom/responsibility. My friend started on one side and included the other. I started on the opposite side, but also included the other. As we talked through our positions, we discovered that we were embracing the same truths from the Scriptures. It was fun to make this discovery rather than to have jumped to erroneous conclusions about each other's biblical soundness.

Cutting sarcasm has no place in dialogue. The humor of Christ makes use of irony, but not sarcasm. "The ironical is always marked with a subtle sharpness of insight, free from the desire to wound."[1] *Free from the desire to wound* is a good test for determining the wholesomeness of our humor.

The Christian has another reason for not coming at life with somberness. Although he may experience tragedies in the present, his future has in it ultimate triumph. Christ said, "In the world you have tribulation; but be of good cheer, I have overcome the world."[2]

Lord, free us from taking ourselves so seriously and give us the grace to laugh heartily and love courageously!

Questions for Personal Reflection and Group Interaction

1. On a scale from 0 to 10, which number would you pick to represent the amount of humor in your life?
2. Have you ever viewed God as having a beautiful sense of humor?
3. Have you ever tried to bluff another person?
4. Is anyone bluffing you?
5. Have you learned how to laugh at yourself?
6. Can you permit others the freedom to be different from you?
7. When you state your viewpoint, is it to state your convictions for your own benefit, or are you really concerned that the other person understand your view?
8. Is your humor sarcastic?
9. Can you celebrate the gift of life in the midst of your conflicts and struggles?

8. Prayer — A Neglected Resource

A CHAPTER ON PRAYER may suggest to many that we are moving away from practical solutions toward devotional suggestions which can have real meaning only for the supersaints. Not so! What God does in the life of the one praying, as well as in the life of the one prayed for, makes prayer our most valuable resource for resolving conflicts. This is especially true when we are serious about communicating with God and seeking His solution for our predicament.

There are many ways of deluding ourselves into thinking that we are praying when actually we are not. Following are three typical substitutes for prayer. Too often we simply try to make God see things our way and use Him as an added club for bringing the other person around to our position. When this happens, the usual outcome is increased contempt for the person using such tactics and a deep distrust of his religious experience.

Another condition that can arise when we are under great stress is our focusing so much attention on our crisis that we actually end up praying to our problem instead of to God. When our problem becomes bigger than God in our minds, we really are in trouble. That kind of prayer only increases our anxiety and leaves us with a sense of hopelessness. If our plight is greater than God, what hope is there?

Another block to authentic communication with "the God who is there" comes when we focus unrealistically on ourselves. Christ illustrated this truth in His story of the two men who went to the temple to pray.[1] "The Pharisee stood and prayed thus with himself, God, I thank thee, that I am not as other men are, extortioners, unjust, adulterers, or even as this publican. I fast twice in the week, I give tithes of all that I possess." He thought too highly of himself. He *was* as other men are! So are we all. We may be strong in one aspect in which another is weak, but we all have our weaknesses and our blind spots. Although the Pharisee boasted of his morals and his religious practices, his very boasting revealed a greater weakness — pride.

The other man in the story was aware of his true condition. "And the publican, standing afar off, would not lift up so much as his eyes unto heaven, but smote upon his breast, saying, God be merciful to me a sinner." The Lord concluded His story thus: "I tell you, this man went down to his house justified rather than the other: for every one that exalteth himself shall be abased; and he that humbleth himself shall be exalted."

When the Lord convicts us of our weaknesses, He opens the door for tolerance and understanding on our part of the foibles of others. Casting stones comes easily when we are out of touch with our own needs and brokenness.

The primary focus of prayer is God. The very act of looking to Him for help takes our attention away from ourselves, from each other, and from the distressful situation which exists. In that moment of openness God may give us insight, understanding, compassion, quietness of spirit, and confidence that the situation can be worked out. Isaiah said it beautifully — "But they that wait upon the LORD shall renew their strength; they shall mount up with wings as eagles; they shall run, and not be weary; and they shall walk, and not faint."[2]

What do we see when we focus our attention on God? Some may see an extension of their father's image, and God to them is as kind or as harsh as their parent may have been. Others may see God as someone or something vague or mysterious without definable dimensions. To others, God may be like some minister who left a deep impression upon them. One little boy said of a prominent pastor in our city, "God came by to see us!"

Jesus Christ is our clearest revelation of God. In Him we can truly say, "God came by to see us!" The Gospels give us ample information and illustrations about Him — His character, His attitudes, His actions, His message. Their purpose is to introduce us to Him that we too might believe — and by believing, experience His transforming love in our own lives.

Read Matthew, Mark, Luke, and John in the New Testament with this question in mind: What is God like as He is revealed in Jesus Christ? I am convinced you will come away with the profound impression that *God loves you and has a magnificent purpose for you in spite of what you have been or done in the past.* Unless we see God in this light, the only other motivation left for praying to Him is desperation — grasping at a straw.

His love refuses to coerce you into faith. He draws you toward Himself, but never does He violate your will. The message of Joshua to the Hebrew people applies to us today: "Choose you this day whom you will serve."[3]

When we pray, focusing our attention on Christ, God does become bigger than our plight and He can enable us to find a viable solution to our problem.

Prayer, as a pouring out of our deepest self to God and as an attitude of openness and receptivity to God, allows Him to bring our will more into harmony with His will. This transition from the I-want-my-way attitude to the I-want-life-as-You-meant-it-to-be-Lord posture may come in a moment, or it may come only after great struggle. But when it comes, we will know the power of God to change, to heal, and to reconcile. The Lord knew the liberation that would come and the power that would be set in motion when He told His disciples to "pray for them which despitefully use you. . . ."[4]

I must bear witness that the single most effective resource I have found for resolving conflict is prayer. Two very strong men locked horns in my last pastorate. They were quite capable of severely rupturing the fellowship of the church. Neither seemed open to reconciliation. I spent one whole morning in prayer over the situation. The conflict was so explosive that I knew there was only one pathway to pacification: that was for one or both to swallow some pride and be willing to build a bridge over to the other instead of stubbornly digging deeper in his own conviction. I knew my attitude had to be accepting of them as persons and that I must acknowledge in some way, not only my awareness of their strong feelings in the situation, but also my concern over how they were affecting the church body.

Shortly after lunch I went to Ray's home. We took a walk together and began to talk about where we were in this impasse. After a couple of hours of wrestling with himself, Ray wanted to visit Jim. We went together to Jim's. I cannot tell you how different Jim's attitude was. It was as though someone else had given Jim permission to work through his feelings and had helped him regain his perspective. I am convinced *Someone* else had! Needless to say, Ray and Jim had a beautiful experience of reconciliation and became close friends as a result of this encounter.

The next time you are faced with a conflict try your own experiment in prayer. First, ask the Lord to help you be honest with Him about your feelings. Second, ask Him to help you see your weaknesses as well as your strengths in the situation. Next, ask Him to give you a love for the person or persons involved in the conflict — i.e., a genuine concern for their welfare. Then, ask Him for the courage and the wisdom to install the first board on the bridge of reconciliation. Remember the Lord's words: "Blessed are the peacemakers: for they shall be called the children of God."[5]

Questions for Personal Reflection and Group Interaction

1. Is prayer a significant resource for you in handling conflict? If not, what resources do you use?
2. What is the primary focus of prayer?
3. Have you ever experienced a change either in yourself or in another that you attributed to *answered prayer?* Share.

4. Do you really want to see things God's way, or entreat Him to see things your way? What do you do with that *seemingly* overpowering tendency to use God for your own purposes?

5. Have you ever felt so overwhelmed by your problems that they seemed bigger than God? (Despair overshadowing hope is an indication that our problems are getting the best of us.)

6. Would you be willing to make a thirty-day experiment with prayer? Begin praying daily about the aspects of need in your own life, in the life of your spouse, your children, and some friends. Examine the content of the prayer Christ taught His disciples to pray in Matthew 6:9-13.

9. Forgiveness — An Essential Ingredient

EVERY RELATIONSHIP of any depth must have in it a generous amount of forgiveness to survive. We all have weaknesses and make immature responses that hurt others. Those closest to us can be and usually are hurt the most by our inadequacies. Therefore the more intimate our relationship, the more essential our capacity to forgive becomes.

Holding a grudge will cause any relationship to deteriorate. The reason is, we tend to interpret all other experiences with that person in the light of their offense. A mild abuse may create only a mild huff; but the more serious the affront, the deeper the resentment.

We can hold a grudge against another because of some outrageous injury, or we can store up a multitude of small wounds. Both produce the same result: once we have an overload of unresolved conflict, it becomes almost impossible to see the offender in a positive light. At this point even the smallest bruise is received as a major assault.

I see the above drama being played out repeatedly in marital conflicts. Too often couples wait until there is little but hurt and hostility left before they see a counselor. It is absolutely amazing how every action by one can be interpreted so negatively by the other. The relationship can become so fragmented that there literally is nothing either can do right. To keep your relationship from reaching this distressing point, or in seeking to recover from such a disintegrating response pattern, *forgiveness must play a major role*. To hoard up rebuffs not only destroys in the end, but makes one miserable along the way.

Just as a developing person must experience love in order to learn how to love, so must we experience forgiveness before we can offer it in any depth. Again, the Christian faith brings to us the resources essential for engaging in the liberating life-style of forgiveness.

We recognize that "normal" human experience carries an awareness of guilt. The person who is incapable of feeling guilt is out of touch with reality and may be described as psychopathic. True, a person experiencing guilt may also be out of touch with reality. He may have an overactive conscience that contributes to the development of a guilt complex. The result will be the feeling of guilt over everything he does, says, or thinks. There is a definite distinction between *false guilt*, assuming blame that does not belong to us; *true guilt*, experiencing the reproofs of a sensitive conscience that is telling it like it is; and *denied guilt*, which takes the attitude of innocence and blames everyone else for all the problems in the world.

The good news of the Christian faith confronts us with the reality of our true guilt. We have gone our own way and have built a kingdom around ourselves and played the role of god within that kingdom. The words used to describe our moral insanity are sin, selfishness, pride, narcissism, rebellion, estrangement, and irresponsibility. The history of man reveals the destructiveness inherent within his nature. It is true that *a man left to himself becomes the enemy of all, including himself.* Apart from the life-transforming experience of Christ there is little hope of any great change for any of us.

I think it is telling and extremely encouraging to find that a noted psychiatrist has written a book entitled *Whatever Became of Sin?* In his book, Karl Menninger points out that "the disappearance of the word 'sin' involves a shift in the allocation of responsibility for evil."[1] Man flees his guilt!

To face up to our rebellion against God and our selfishness toward others demands that we swallow our pride, humble ourselves, repent of our wrongs, and seek God's forgiveness. When we reach such a posture, we discover that we not only receive forgiveness from God through our faith in Christ, but also are given a new life. "When someone becomes a Christian he becomes a brand new person inside. He is not the same any more. A new life has begun!"[2]

Forgiveness in the biblical sense means "lightness or lifting up; remitting; to pardon; or to wipe away." It carries the idea of releasing one from bondage to a past act. When God forgives, He removes the barrier that sin has created between us and Him.

Guilt crushes while forgiveness releases, and how great that release! David describes it best in relating his experience with guilt and forgiveness.

> What happiness for those whose guilt has been forgiven! What joys when sins are covered over! What relief for those who have confessed their sins and God has cleared their record.
>
> There was a time when I wouldn't admit what a sinner I was. But my dishonesty made me miserable and filled my days with frustration. All day and all night your hand was heavy on me. My strength evaporated like water on a sunny day until I finally admitted all my sins to you and stopped trying to hide them. I said to myself, "I will confess them to the Lord." And you forgave me! All my guilt is gone.[3]

The consequences of our rebellion may not be removed, but in the context of God's forgiveness, even the consequences can be used by Him as a redemptive force within us and our world. We do well to learn the reliability of the principle that "whatsoever a man soweth, that shall he also reap,"[4] and to give greater thought to how we are investing our lives.

God's forgiveness comes to us through Jesus Christ. It is in the Cross of Christ that we can by faith realize God's complete forgiveness. Realizing God's forgiveness in Christ is indescribable!

The joy that comes from knowing that we are among the forgiven is a peak experience which profoundly alters our destiny and character.

As Christians we continue to fall short, must confess our sin, and accept Christ's forgiveness to remain in an open, growing posture. One of the best descriptions of this spiritual reality is found in 1 John 1:8,9: "If we say that we have no sin, we deceive ourselves, and the truth is not in us. If we confess our sins, He is faithful and just to forgive us our sins, and to cleanse us from all unrighteousness."

An indication that we have really opened ourselves to Christ's forgiveness is our willingness to make whatever restitution possible toward those who may have been hurt by our actions. Remember the impact that Christ had on Zacchaeus? The Scriptures tell us that "Zacchaeus stood before the Lord and said, 'Sir, from now on I will give half my wealth to the poor, and if I find I have overcharged anyone on his taxes, I will penalize myself by giving him back four times as much!' "[5] What he experienced in the presence of Christ made him a generous man who wanted to make restitution to any of whom he had taken unfair advantage.

The place to start learning forgiveness is with God. Once we have experienced His forgiveness, it becomes easier to acknowledge our wrongs to another and ask their forgiveness. A good test here may come in the form of a question. How hard is it for you to say, "I am sorry" or "Please forgive me for being so insensitive"?

If you are the offended party, how easy is it for you to forgive? *The more profound your own experience of being forgiven, the easier it will be for you to extend forgiveness to another.* Some persons believe you cannot forgive another unless the offender asks for your forgiveness. This may be true for genuine healing of the relationship, but from the biblical perspective, forgiveness must be extended regardless. Christ said, "Whenever you stand praying, forgive, if you have anything against any one; so that your Father also who is in heaven may forgive you your trespasses."[6] If our fists are tightly clenched around a grudge, how can we receive into our hands the marvelous gift of God's forgiveness?

Forgiveness is expensive! For God to extend forgiveness to us, it cost Him His Son on a cross. It is costly as well for us to offer forgiveness to another. When we have been hurt, something within us wants to hurt back, retaliate, and extract payment. It's hard to get free of our hostility and our resentment, especially if it is obvious that the offender has deliberately taken advantage of us. Yet we must recognize that we are the custodians of our own dignity and the dignity of others, but not the avenger of its outrage. This insight may give us a clue as to how we can extend authentic forgiveness, which will be emotionally and spiritually healthy for us and hopefully redemptive for the offender.

The Christian is not called to let the world run over him. Christ furnishes us the model which allows us to see this concept in action. The Pharisees refused to open themselves to the person, the miracles, or the teachings of Christ, because He did not fit their preconceived mold of what the Messiah would be and do. They watched Him like wolves ready for the kill at any opportunity. Finally Christ confronted them with their deficiencies, and we have His strong confrontation recorded in Matthew 23. Christ said of them,

> You would think these Jewish leaders and these Pharisees were Moses, the way they keep making up so many laws! And of course you should obey their every whim! It may be all right to do what they say, but above anything else, don't follow their example. For they don't do what they tell you to do. They load you with impossible demands that they themselves don't even try to keep.
>
> Everything they do is done for show. . . . Woe to you, Pharisees, and you other religious leaders. Hypocrites! For you won't let others enter the Kingdom of Heaven, and won't go in yourselves.[7]

The chapter goes on, but this statement is sufficient to point out the necessity of making your feelings known to clear the air. This is honesty spoken in love! Christ could confront others from the position of strength because He was perfect. We must remember that our confrontation with another comes from a degree of weakness, because we are not perfect. The other person could, if he had all the facts about us, turn and confront us with our own faults. This fact demands even more that our honest expressions of negative feelings be given in an *attitude of humility.* Our statements of hurt or resentment should be an effort to let the other person know where we are and how we feel about what he has said or done. Our assertion should not be an attack aimed at getting even with an enemy. *amen*

Sometimes this kind of honest confrontation is essential

before we can release our resentment and extend forgiveness. We may have misunderstood the intent of the other, and this opening would give him a chance to explain himself and enable us to understand the situation from his perspective. Often simple understanding will dissolve the conflict immediately. But if the other person did intend to hurt us and makes that intent known, then the confrontation will have given us some honest release that will help us keep our balance and enable us to go on, to accept the affront as the other person's problem and to seek God's resources for forgiving and living with the situation until something changes. It is important to remember that *we make matters worse when we take on the other person's problem as our own.* There is no way to keep his problem from affecting us; the closer the person is to us, the more we will be affected. But by not assuming his problem, we can survive better while giving him time either to resolve his inner conflict or to become willing to work out the conflict with us.

Forgiveness opens the door to understanding and removes the ensuing bitterness. It is important for all involved that we ask the living Christ to enable us to forgive those who may be acting at a given moment as our enemies.

Questions for Personal Reflection and Group Interaction

1. Are you currently harboring any resentments? If so, are they affecting any of your attitudes or actions, and in what way?
2. Have you ever experienced letting go of a grudge you were holding? What was it like?
3. Can you recognize the tendency in yourself to interpret others' actions negatively when you are in conflict with them?
4. How do you handle rebuffs?
5. Have you ever experienced forgiveness from another as an undeserved gift from him to you? What was your response?
6. Have you ever given another forgiveness as an undeserved gift from you to him? How did that make you feel? What was his response?
7. Can you recognize the difference between *true guilt* and *false guilt*?
8. Have you ever faced up to your rebellion against God and your selfishness toward others? Share.
9. What do you do with guilt?

10. Have you ever experienced God's forgiveness?
11. Have you learned how to express negative feelings in a nonjudgmental fashion?
12. Is it easy or hard for you to offer forgiveness? to receive forgiveness?

PART TWO

Confronting Conflict
in Relationships

Your own soul is nourished when you are kind; it is destroyed when you are cruel.

— Proverbs 11:17
The Living Bible

Some people like to make cutting remarks, but the words of the wise soothe and heal.

— 12:18

Reliable communication permits progress.

— 13:17b

If you profit from constructive criticism you will be elected to the wise men's hall of fame. But to reject criticism is to harm yourself and your own best interests.

— 15:31,32

Love forgets mistakes; nagging about them parts the best of friends.

— 17:9

Open rebuke is better than hidden love.
Wounds from a friend are better than kisses from an enemy!

— 27:5,6

10. Working With Someone You Don't Like

FEW PEOPLE WILL ever be able to say with Will Rogers, "I never met a man I didn't like." Now, whether Will would have felt the same if he had worked forty hours a week beside certain persons is purely speculative, but he probably would not.

Most of us have been or will be put in situations — either vocationally or on a short-term basis, with someone who rubs us the wrong way. This is normal. After all, to suppose that everyone we meet will like us is a bit egotistical; to demand of ourselves that we enjoy everyone we meet is a bit unreasonable. We can come to value and respect human life so deeply that we desire the best for everyone we meet. But to have affinity with everyone is unrealistic.

Personality clashes as well as major divergencies of values, tastes, views, and objectives may keep us from enjoying another's company. Within the normal flow of social interaction this usually does not create a severe crisis. A close working relationship with that individual, however, causes the aspects of difference to become magnified. If we happen to need that person's approval, the battle we fight is usually with ourselves — we do what he expects or wants, and we resent ourselves for doing it. On the other hand, the less we care for or need that approval, the more straightforward we are in expressing our differences.

This person could be our boss or an employee or a member of the same club or church. But here we have it — a clash with a person with whom we must associate, at least for a time. What do we do? What are you doing?

1. It is important that we identify the situation we are in and examine our own responses and feelings to see what we are doing with it. We may be storing up resentment, or we may be taking it out on someone to whom it does not belong, such as our spouse or children. We may be hitting at the person who irritates us with unkind remarks or cutting him down in the eyes of others. Or we could be indifferent toward him and emotionally respond as if he did not exist. Whatever we are doing, we need to know.

2. We need to ask ourselves "Why?" Why does he irritate me so? Does he remind me of someone else who gave me a hard time, or is he a threat to me because he is so much like me or so opposite? Is it a clash of personalities, of values, of goals, or what? Is he a threat because I sense he does not like me, or maybe he is out to discredit me or get my position?

One hard-driving businessman told me he had been fired from every job he ever had except his present one, in which he was the top man. He said that the day he went to work in all his other jobs, he went after his boss's position. Is it little wonder that his bosses looked for ways to get rid of him? Ambition can be good, but too much can be self-defeating.

Another man shared with me that he really did not like another person who happened to be moving in his circle. I asked him why not. He said he did not know. I then asked him if it could be because they were so much alike. His protest revealed the truth: as it turned out, they were so much alike that they could not tolerate each other. Sometimes we fight most vehemently in others the things we dislike in ourselves.

3. Ask yourself if there is a better way to handle the situation. Sometimes you may need to sit down with the person and

talk out your feelings. This is usually the best approach, unless the other person will not allow any communication to transpire on this level. Then you may need to talk with someone who will keep your conversation confidential and who can help you work through your feelings and enable you to gain some objectivity in the situation.

4. Along with the above steps, ask the living Christ to work in you and in the other person to help you both achieve a creative relationship. Allow some time for this to occur while you attempt to be the person Christ would want you to be in the situation.

5. Recognize that you do not have to be bosom buddies to learn to work together. The relationship may never become ideal, but you both may be able to function in a complementary way while recognizing your unresolved differences. Most people have to operate on this level.

6. The Lord may choose to use this conflict to teach you how to love the unlovely. If you become convinced that this is His assignment, the entire situation takes on the kind of meaning that may enable you to make something beautiful of it.

7. The Lord could be using the conflict to move you in another direction. Dissatisfaction makes it easier to take the risks involved in making a move. You will have to seek God's will for you in this matter diligently. Not that God wants to keep His will for us a secret — He wants to help us understand ourselves better and trust Him more fully. One practical approach is to ask the Lord to open an opportunity to you that would excite you if He desires to move you. He is able to give us both the desire and the opportunity. "For God is at work within you, helping you want to obey Him, and then helping you do what He wants."[1]

There is no foolproof method for determining with absolute certainty the correct course of action in our conflicts. Desiring to do the "right" thing does not eliminate the faith-risk involved in deciding what God is saying to us in the midst of our struggle. The good news of the gospel is that no mistake is fatal except the failure to venture with Him. It is as we venture with Him that He is able to correct and redeem our mistakes.

Questions for Personal Reflection
and Group Interaction

1. Identify one or more individuals with whom you clash. (Keep their identities anonymous for group sharing.) What bothers you about them?
2. Do you have any idea what bothers them about you?
3. How are you handling the situation? Is it working, or making matters worse?
4. Could you be fighting in that other person a problem of your own?
5. Are you having difficulty understanding the other person, or do you understand all too well?
6. Have you ever tried to *talk through* your differences with the other person? If so, what was his response? Why do you think he responded as he did?
7. What positive things can you learn from your conflict? What positive things have you learned?

11. Living With an Alcoholic

PERSONAL CONFLICT will arise when there exists an abnormal problem such as alcoholism. Improving our own interaction patterns should remain one of our primary goals, but the greatest improvement in the world will be insufficient for effecting recovery when dealing with this disease.

Alcoholism has existed since man first crushed a grape, yet its cause and its cure still evade us. And it does not affect the alcoholic alone. The circle of tragedy encompasses the lives of all those closely involved, and they may actually be caught up in the sickness themselves.

Dr. Roger Egeberg of the U. S. Department of Health, Education and Welfare has labeled alcoholism the number one public health problem in our nation. Nine million Americans are affected directly, as well as another thirty-six million family members. Sociologist Walter S. Krusich gives statistical evidence that if twelve people begin to drink together socially, one will become an alcoholic within ten years and three others will end up with serious drinking problems.[1]

95

Dr. William B. TerHune, a nationally respected authority, has warned that if the present trend continues, one of every eight adult Americans now living will become an alcoholic. The problem is staggering and creates untold pain for all whom it touches.

Only 3 percent of the nation's alcoholics end up on skid row. That means 97 percent remain to some degree in the main flow of society. Alcoholics occupy all levels of public office; fly our airplanes; perform surgery; police our streets; teach our children; and even preach in our pulpits. Therefore, being on skid row is not a test for determining whether a person is an alcoholic.

The question "How can I know if he or she² is an alcoholic?" is asked repeatedly of ministers, counselors, and sympathetic friends. It is highly important, therefore, that we are sufficiently well-informed to recognize the disease so that we might be a part of the solution rather than a part of the problem.

Alcoholism is a triple disease. It involves a physical dysfunction in that the victim cannot ingest alcohol with control. It involves a personality structure especially vulnerable to stress. Finally, because the inroads of alcohol are superimposed on the personality, the alcoholic is a spiritually sick person as well. In other words, *alcoholism is a physical allergy to alcohol coupled with a mental obsession to use it, which results in a sickness of the total person.* The "allergy" is frequently likened to diabetes. For reasons unknown, the diabetic has lost the ability to handle sugar as other people do, and the loss is permanent. The alcoholic has lost, for the rest of his life, the ability to handle alcohol. Never again will he be able to return to moderate drinking.

Yet the alcoholic sees drinking as the solution and not the problem. For him, alcohol furnishes a shortcut to overcoming shyness, easing a crisis, soothing a conscience, subduing anger and resentment, creating a feeling of genius, justifying failure, shrugging off lost opportunities, enjoying self-pity, ignoring responsibilities, and pushing facts aside. The alcoholic gets drunk instead of facing life. If one or more major adjustments in living — such as health, vocation, or social or marital relationships — are periodically or continuously hampered by drinking, the evidence would indicate the presence of alcoholism.

Many myths concerning alcoholism have no foundation in fact. Being alcoholic has nothing to do with the time of day or how much one drinks; where or how often; with whom he drinks or what type of beverage. The crucial question is, What is alcohol doing to the person?

Authorities in the field identify two main distinctions between the heavy drinker and the alcoholic.

First, the alcoholic builds up a tolerance to alcohol, which means that his capacity for alcohol increases and it constantly takes more alcohol to have an effect on him. In the heavy drinker, the same amount of alcohol generally produces the same effect; if he drinks more than he usually does, he is affected more. Secondly, someone who is a heavy drinker and not an alcoholic can choose where, when, how much, and with whom he drinks; he can drink or not, as he likes. In short, he has control over his drinking. With the alcoholic, it's the other way around.[3]

But the experts are quick to point out that the heavy drinker may actually be in the first stages of alcoholism. The American Medical Association stated:

Alcoholism can be classified into (1) primary alcoholism, which includes (a) those patients who from the very first drink of an alcoholic beverage are unable to control their desire for it and (b) those who through use over a great many years have developed an inability to take a drink or leave it alone and have become like group (a) and (2) secondary alcoholism, which includes those who use alcohol for its sedative action as a means of escape from reality and, in particular, from their personal problems. . . . This secondary group comprise by far the majority of patients suffering from alcoholism; however, most alcoholic patients prefer to be in the primary group.[4]

For either classification, one factor holds true: alcoholism is a *progressive* disease. Although it may take from five to twenty-five years for the "secondary alcoholic" to develop recognizable symptoms, the downward spiral continues its relentless course. Some may pause for years at one stage or another. Others will go through the stages with greater rapidity. All, however, will arrive at the fork in the road: one avenue leads to recovery, the other to insanity or death.

There does not exist a general type of alcoholic. There are almost as many patterns as there are alcoholics. For our purposes we will examine three types — *steady, periodic,* and *plateau* drinkers. As the word suggests, the "steady alcoholic" is one who drinks continuously but who may have intermittent periods of more intense or "binge" drinking. The "periodic drinker" usually abstains between binges, but the interludes tend to become shorter through the years. The "plateau drinker" does not seek the maximum effects of alcohol; he simply needs to maintain a certain medium level of inebriation at all times. The plateau drinker may ration his supply in order to distribute its effects over a longer period of time.

If you think you may be becoming addicted to alcohol, ask yourself the following questions:

1. Do you lose time from work due to drinking?
2. Is drinking making your home life unhappy?
3. Do you drink because you are shy with other people?
4. Is drinking affecting your reputation?
5. Have you ever felt remorse after drinking?
6. Have you gotten into financial difficulties as a result of drinking?
7. Do you turn to lower companions and an inferior environment when you drink?
8. Does your drinking make you careless of your family's welfare?
9. Has your ambition decreased since drinking?
10. Do you crave a drink at times?
11. Has your efficiency decreased since drinking?
12. Is drinking jeopardizing your job or business?
13. Do you drink to escape from worries or troubles?
14. Do you drink alone?
15. Have you ever had a complete loss of memory as a result of drinking?
16. Has your physician ever treated you for drinking?
17. Do you drink to build up your self-confidence?
18. Have you ever been to a hospital or institution on account of drinking?[5]

A "yes" answer to two or three of these is a warning that trouble is ahead. There are weaknesses, however, in any list which purposes to evoke self-recognition. A major factor is that the alcoholic is a master of self-deception and, as such, does not recognize alcohol as the cause of the problems listed. The alcoholic may use the list in a negative fashion by picking out a half-dozen or so questions which do not fit his particular style of addiction and use them as proof that he does not have a problem.

Alcoholics Anonymous names some other methods of self-denial and experimentation:

Drinking beer only, limiting the number of drinks, never drinking alone, never drinking in the morning, drinking only at home, never having it in the house, never drinking during business hours, drinking only at parties, switching from scotch to brandy, drinking only natural wines, agreeing to resign if ever drunk on the job, taking a trip, not taking a trip, swearing off forever (with and without a solemn oath), taking more physical exercise, reading inspirational books, going to health farms and sanitariums, accepting voluntary commitment to asylums — we could increase the list ad infinitum.[6]

There is no *cure* for alcoholism. An alcoholic's drinking career is characterized by countless vain attempts to prove that he can drink like other people. No person likes to think he is physically and mentally different from others. The idea that somehow, someday he will control and enjoy his drinking is the great obsession of every abnormal drinker.

The delusion that the alcoholic can control his drinking has to be smashed. Over any considerable period the alcoholic gets worse, never better. Yet, by every form of self-deception and experimentation, the alcoholic will try to prove himself the exception to the rule. Without seeming to care, he will drag all those close to him along in his downward spiral. The fact is that self-knowledge alone will not enable an alcoholic to stop drinking. Without the help of God and caring persons, few are restored to health and happiness. No real alcoholic *ever* regains control. "Absolute abstinence" is the second meaning of "A.A."

There may be a multitude of reasons why a person takes his first drink, but once the drink takes him, *the primary objective in treatment must be to free him from alcohol.* He must be off the booze before he can respond to anything or anyone.

It is important for the nonalcoholic to be reminded that the alcoholic's drinking is compulsive. Because of the nature of a compulsion — most people, including alcoholics, think of their pet compulsions as normal — it is truly difficult for the alcoholic to see his behavior as abnormal. It is also necessary to realize that by the time the alcoholic reaches the stage of addition, *he has organized his personality and his life around alcohol*. Becoming abstinent is not a matter of giving up a bad habit; it is, in fact, giving up the core around which a person has organized his life. The threat of alcohol becoming unavailable produces the same kind of panic in the alcoholic that the removal of oxygen would produce in another person. So even if a person recognizes in himself early signs of dependence on alcohol, he normally rationalizes and says, "These warning signs don't apply to me. I have very good reasons for my drinking behavior. I can quit when I want to." The fact is that when an alcoholic can stop, he usually doesn't want to; and when he wants to, he can't.

Why does the alcoholic rationalize and resist the idea that he might be an alcoholic? The answer lies in part in that he lives in a culture which traditionally has regarded inebriety as a matter of morals and will power. Despite all that research has revealed and all that case studies have documented to prove that alcoholism is a compulsion and a disease, most people still believe otherwise. No matter what we say, we still really believe that if he *really* wanted to stop drinking, he would simply stop.

This lack of acceptance of the sickness concept is naturally internalized by the alcoholic. As long as he thinks of his trouble as essentially a matter of will power, he will resist outside help. In his mind, to seek help would be an admission that he is weak and morally corrupt. Once he accepts the sickness concept, however, and applies it to himself he will be more inclined to get help.

If we in the Christian community continue to perpetuate the moralistic concept of alcoholism, we will be responsible in part for pushing alcoholics deeper into the dark morass. As Marty Mann, founder of the National Council on Alcoholism, puts the matter:

> Up to now the alcoholic has been made to feel shame if he could not handle his drinking by himself. Our goal must be to reverse that: to make him feel shame at not seeking help for his illness. If he

really comes to believe that he has a disease, the chances are greatly enhanced that he will seek treatment for it. Thousands of cases have proved this.[7]

To help, we must clearly understand the point Carroll A. Wise made when he wrote, "Fundamentally, the alcoholic is not sick because he drinks but . . . he drinks because he is sick, and then becomes doubly sick."[8]

The alcoholic has two primary defenses — denial and projection. He denies that he has a problem until long after it is painfully noticeable to others. Since we have dealt with his denial more fully in the earlier part of this chapter, we will focus here on his second defense — projection. He often projects what he hates about himself on those who figure prominently in his life — his wife, his children, or his boss. What he says about them is a clue to what he feels about himself. Thus the pain and destruction of alcoholism are not limited to alcoholics alone. Around each alcoholic there is what has been fittingly termed "a circle of tragedy," comprising all those whose lives are in close touch with the alcoholic's.

One lady wrote to me concerning her crisis of living with an alcoholic.

> The first day it begins to dawn on you that you could be living with an alcoholic, the immediate reaction is to reject it — bury it — assume you are the one who is a little tense about alcohol yourself. . . . For seven years I pretended it was not a problem. I retreated into the unreal assumption that this was normal living. . . . My husband believed that he was not an alcoholic because he had never been in jail or had to take a morning drink. Still our marriage and home were in a constant state of tension. Everything and everybody were blamed for his lack of happiness except the bottle. Well-meaning friends gave advice to no avail, and even involvement in church activities did not lessen the problem. I began to feel like I might be crazy myself. . . . One day a good friend, herself a recovered alcoholic, said to me, "I can't help you. You either stay in this mess because you like it or because you are afraid of a change." Those were tough but sobering words from a friend.

A drinking problem often can be more easily recognized by the wife's behavior than by the drinker's. Once she starts covering up for him and shielding him from as many of the consequences of his habit as she can, she is only helping to prolong the drinking years and the agony that goes along with them. The truth is, an alcoholic could not go on drinking as he does if his wife (or mother) would allow him to stand on his own feet and accept full responsibility for his actions.

Pastor Paul, author of *The 13th American* and a recovered alcoholic, says that *the most cruel thing that can be done to the alcoholic is to allow him to evade his problem.* He needs to be confronted with the problem in an understanding, nonjudgmental manner. To gain understanding, the spouse or boss or friend should get some facts on alcoholism. These are readily available from a local Alcoholics Anonymous or Alanon group, or by writing A.A. World Services, Inc., P.O. Box 459, Grand Central Station, New York, NY 10017.

The alcoholic must "hit bottom" before he will seriously seek help. The terms "high bottom" and "low bottom" refer to the degree of social disintegration that has occurred by the time he becomes open to receiving help. By withdrawing the props and protection, the bottom can be elevated more quickly for the alcoholic, which is obviously the loving thing to do. It is counterproductive to pamper an alcoholic who is still drinking. He must not be shielded from the consequences of his behavior. He must be accepted as a sick person, but as Gert Behanna, author of *The Late Liz*, said, "Do not accept our unacceptable behavior." The nonalcoholic spouse must not assume blame for all that goes wrong in an alcoholic marriage. No person ever made another person alcoholic, and no person can "unmake" him as such.

Following is a list of dos and don'ts that may aid recovery:

DO learn the facts about alcoholism.
DO develop an attitude to match the facts.
DO talk to someone who understands alcoholism.
DO take a personal inventory of yourself.
DO go to [A.A. or Alanon].
DO maintain a healthy atmosphere in your home.
DO encourage your husband's (or wife's) new interests.
DO take a relapse lightly if there is one.
DO pass on your knowledge of alcoholism to others.
DON'T preach and lecture to the alcoholic.
DON'T have a "holier-than-thou" attitude.
DON'T use the "if you loved me" appeal.
DON'T make threats you won't carry out.

DON'T hide liquor or pour it out.
DON'T argue with the alcoholic during a drunk.
DON'T make an issue over the treatment.
DON'T expect an immediate, 100 percent recovery.
DON'T be jealous of recovery methods.
DON'T try to protect the drinker from alcohol. [9]

An A.A. friend writes,

> Most of us alcoholics try to hide our problems from ourselves, and most of us receive help in hiding from those who love us and try to protect us. Unfortunately, this protection only prevents us from seeking and receiving the help we so desperately need.

There is hope and help for the alcoholic today and for the alcoholic's family, who usually need help as much as the alcoholic himself. A.A., Alanon, and Alateen have by far the best track record for helping the alcoholic and his family back to health and sanity. Neither medicine, psychiatry, nor the clergy have been able to effect more than a 1 percent rate of recovery; yet the most conservative figures relating to A.A. indicate more than 60 percent of those who stay in the program recover. Thus A.A. statistically is sixty times more effective than any other known approach to the problem! That is so significant, that anyone who really wants help has by far the greatest chance of finding it in the A.A. program.

One reason for the success of A.A. is that the program treats the whole person — body, mind, and spirit. Alcoholics Anonymous is the oldest (forty years), largest (850,000 members, i.e., recovering alcoholics), and the most successful organization in existence for helping the alcoholic. There is no mystery or magic about A.A. Its simple program of recovery was first lived, then written by two "hopeless alcoholics" — Bill W. and Dr. Bob.

The A.A. program comprises twelve *suggested* steps for recovery, and it emphasizes grace and freedom. The program is deeply spiritual and has such realistic guidelines for recovery that they would produce a healthy way of life for anyone. I cannot count all the people I know who have found Jesus Christ as their personal Savior while working through the A.A. steps. Some of our Christian Concern Fellowship meetings could just as easily be A.A. meetings, there are so many A.A.'s present. I am truly grateful for my A.A.

friends: they have recovered from a living hell, and consequently they deeply understand grace, forgiveness, acceptance, and love.

The twelve-step program, with appropriate modifications, can be used by anyone seeking a more successful, meaningful way of life.

1. We admitted we were powerless over alcohol — that our lives had become unmanageable.
2. Came to believe that a Power greater than ourselves could restore us to sanity.
3. Made a decision to turn our will and our lives over to the care of God as we understood Him.
4. Made a searching and fearless moral inventory of ourselves.
5. Admitted to God, to ourselves, and to another human being the exact nature of our wrongs.
6. Were entirely ready to have God remove all these defects of character.
7. Humbly asked Him to remove our shortcomings.
8. Made a list of all persons we had harmed and became willing to make amends to them all.
9. Made direct amends to such people wherever possible, except when to do so would injure them or others.
10. Continued to take personal inventory and when we were wrong promptly admitted it.
11. Sought through prayer and meditation to improve our conscious contact with God as we understood Him, praying only for knowledge of His will for us and the power to carry that out.
12. Having had a spiritual awakening as the result of these steps, we tried to carry this message to alcoholics, and to practice these principles in all our affairs. [10]

A close friend, a member of A.A., once gave me a copy of their *Serenity Prayer*.

God grant me the serenity to accept the things I cannot change, courage to change the things I can, and the wisdom to know the difference.

These simple words have been a "lifeline" to many struggling alcoholics. They can also make a real difference in the attitudes and responses of those trying to help them. Listen to an alcoholic describe her experience with A.A.

As an active alcoholic, I sought help from family, friends, medical doctors, psychiatrists, the church and *finally*, A.A. I attended A.A. meetings for over three years without showing any signs of recovery. The 12 steps hung on the wall in plain sight, they were verbalized and read from both books and pamphlets. *The answers were there*, but I was incapable of receiving them. Yet, I needed those A.A.'s and their love, acceptance and encouragement in the face of one failure after another, week after week, year after year. I never once felt rejected, judged, or hopeless at an A.A. meeting. They loved me, cared for me, shared with me, and would have fed me, clothed me and housed me had that been my need.

They did not demand that I "shape up or ship out." They did not give me answers and leave me alone to work them out. They identified with me in the midst of my problem, and were true channels of the grace of a loving God.

I don't know where I'd be today if their availability had been dictated by my response to their answers. It took three and one-half years before I could begin to put the principles of the A.A. program into practice in my life. Three and one-half years of having the answers and being unable, or unwilling (what's the difference, I thought I was sincere) to appropriate them. If A.A. had just been principles, I would not have made it. The principles were the answers, but those *people* sustained me with their love until I could take the help they so desperately wanted me to have.

I cannot convey adequately to you the deep respect I have for Alcoholics Anonymous. The organization has learned how to apply the good news of the Judeo-Christian faith to a specific problem, and the results have been phenomenal.

Verdell and I were invited to a dinner party at Jim and Sherry Hutchinson's and heard Roy T. share his story. Roy believes he was an alcoholic from the first time he tasted alcohol. Friends who ran in the same affluent, prep-school crowd in high school recall that his drinking was "outstanding," even in a hard-drinking group. His bizarre behavior even then earned him the nicknames "Wild Man" and "White Trash."

Roy had a spiritual experience in the army in Germany in 1955, which gave him pause for thought about his drinking, but failed to curtail it.

A good job, loving family, material and social advantages only enabled him to continue his progressive addiction. His first marriage ended in divorce.

An introduction to A.A. in 1958, followed by sporadic attendance at meetings — including one year of sobriety during that time — were not effective. He failed to apply the A.A. program to his life.

Finally Roy hit bottom in Mexico City in 1973. A desperate phone call from Roy's wife to a nonalcoholic member of our fellowship in Dallas resulted in another phone call to an A.A. member of our fellowship who "happened" to be in Mexico City. Fifteen minutes later, Roy "heard" the A.A. message for the first time.

Since then, the compulsion to drink has been lifted, and Roy is growing and very active in the A.A. program. He not only considers himself a miracle, but also notices miraculous changes in his wife, who is active in Alanon — a world-wide fellowship for relatives and friends of alcoholics with the expressed purpose of encouraging and helping them to cope effectively with uncontrolled drinking within the family circle.

I knew Roy prior to his sobriety. But the change I saw in him, the enthusiasm he had for life and for people, was beautiful. We listened for more than an hour as Roy shared what A.A. meant to him and how God had found him through their ministry. Truly he was good news to us all!

A.A. is the greatest resource we have for helping an alcoholic, yet it is probably the last place most alcoholics will look for help. The denial syndrome we discussed previously will be one reason he resists A.A., but also, deep down, he knows that this is where the real answer lies and he's not ready for it yet. One honest A.A. member put it this way: "I never wanted to quit drinking; I just wanted to stop getting drunk."

If you think you may be an alcoholic but resist the idea of going to A.A. because of fear of exposure, think again. Most people closely associated with you probably already know. Answer this question for yourself: "Would you rather be known as the town drunk, or a recovering alcoholic?" Besides, people only use their first names at an A.A. meeting, so you can remain anonymous if you choose. *If alcohol has a strong hold on you, go to A.A.!* If it is giving you or others problems, but you do not believe you are an alcoholic, take a test for yourself: *stop drinking!* If you keep rationalizing yourself back to the bottle, you need A.A.

There is something that the nonalcoholic family members and friends can do. You can learn the intelligent way to live with the problem. All too often the nonalcoholics involved begin to react to the alcoholic in anger, frustration, and despair — which only makes matters worse. The alcoholic is locked into his illness, but the nonalcoholic can help to unlock that door by learning new roles and attitudes from those who understand the problem. As long as the alcoholic reacts as the victim and the spouse as the provoker, there is little hope for recovery.

Alanon and Alateen are two organizations that specialize in helping the nonalcoholic family members and friends understand the problems that have been created for them as well as the alcoholic. Alanon's stated purpose is fourfold.

1. To help solve problems due to alcoholism in the home.
2. To share experience, strength, and hope with others in similar circumstances.
3. To improve our own emotional health and spiritual growth.
4. To provide a more wholesome environment for the whole family including the alcoholic, drunk or sober.[11]

A change in the family members' attitudes is often the force for good that finally inspires an alcoholic to seek help. *The alcoholic can be helped whether he wants to be or not!* "Timing" is important. An alcoholic forced into A.A. too soon will simply reject the program and testify to one and all that A.A. does not work for him. A good A.A. member can sense the right time, but a spouse who has really "got" the Alanon program can do the best job of calling in the troops when the time is right. Proper pressures applied by informed family members will have real value in pushing the alcoholic toward help. Would you sit idly by and watch someone you love die of any other disease? Alanon can help you change your attitudes and teach you how to cope with the situation creatively as an informed person, giving you the support you need at this time. One lady wrote:

A friend who knew that I was struggling with an alcoholic husband suggested that I attend an Alanon meeting. I reluctantly agreed to go to one meeting with a person I did not know nor want to know. Going meant facing the problem I had feared and denied for years.

The lady who took me kept telling me I needed to attend at least six meetings consecutively to understand the program. But I didn't want to be at that one meeting. The people were friendly but the program seemed strange and unfamiliar. They talked about accepting what I could not understand and living only for 24 hours at a time.

I did not go back. I was uncomfortable and I did not like that. That was early in the summer of our 21st year of marriage. By November of the same year I was close to breaking. I could not live with the guilt, fear and frustration even as a Christian. I promised God and myself I would go back to Alanon for two meetings a week the entire month of November. I went alone — I needed to go alone because this was not a social occasion, but *a life and death matter.* I listened at the meetings. I found a common bond there with these people, many of whom were living with active alcoholics and were coping with their situation quite well. I sensed I belonged, although I still wanted to reject the problem, the people and the program. But I stayed. By the end of that month I began to let a little of the program sink in. They lived by the Twelve-Step program of A.A. They came to the meetings not to gain sobriety for the alcoholic they were living with, but for serenity for themselves. It is possible to be serene instead of unreasonable and irritable in an alcoholic marriage!

I came to see that I did not cause my husband to become an alcoholic and I could not control or cure his alcoholism. But I could help myself, my children and my alcoholic husband.

I began to refuse to cover for him or assume his responsibilities. This was hard after so many years of doing it the other way. I began to see that his drinking was not a rejection of me but rather a surrender to his compulsion and addiction. I began to release him.

I listed on paper all my fears and went over them with God and with a friend. In facing them they did not appear so huge.

I committed myself to help the alcoholic I was married to, to hit a bottom, if not *the* bottom.

The Alanon slogan is to "Live and Let Live" but before we can "let live" we must first "live." I found that Alanon will help you live in spite of the presence of the disease of alcoholism.

It would seem that nonalcoholic spouses, parents, other relatives, and friends resist going to Alanon or Alateen for some of the very same reasons the alcoholic resists A.A. *If you want him to get help, why don't you get it first?*

Alateen, as we have mentioned, is an organization for young people between the ages of thirteen and twenty who have parents with serious drinking problems. It helps the teen-ager understand the problem and gain some degree of emotional detachment from the parent's problem.

You can call a local A.A. group for information about any of these three organizations.

There is hope for everyone involved in the problem! A.A. states, "Rarely have we seen a person fail who has thoroughly followed our path." That's quite a statement, and their membership comprises thousands of recovered alcoholics who are living proof of its veracity.

Questions for Personal Reflection and Group Interaction

1. Do you have a drinking problem? Would anyone else think you have a drinking problem? Why, or why not?
2. Do you know someone who has a drinking problem? How are you responding to him? Are you in a position to help? From the suggestions in this chapter what do you think you can do which will be most helpful?
3. If one of your family members or someone you are closely associated with has a drinking problem, would you seriously consider visiting an Alanon meeting? From this chapter, what have you learned about the kind of help you can expect from Alanon?
4. What insights have you gained from your study of the problem of alcoholism that will be helpful in dealing with other problems?
5. Are there any aspects of your life that the application of the twelve steps would help?
6. If you think you are an alcoholic, would you be willing to go to an A.A. meeting or at least talk with an A.A. member? Call a local A.A. club, and it will put you in touch with someone and will give you their meeting times.

12. Coping With Emotional Disturbances

SOMETIMES THE ROOT of personal conflict may actually be an emotional imbalance. We are wise to realize that we all behave irrationally at times. The stress of the moment, allowing ourselves to become emotionally overloaded, or being physically exhausted may produce unwarranted hostility, damaging criticisms, and unreasonable behavior. Normally these are short-lived. Once we regain our emotional equilibrium, we return to a more realistic posture.

Although we consciously need to work on altering any and all destructive reaction patterns, be they ever so short-lived, there is no cause for great alarm unless they begin to move beyond our control. Sometimes simply recognizing how ridiculous and unproductive our negative responses are may be enough to motivate a corrective course. Or seeing ourselves in others, especially in our children, may give us a strong push in the right direction. A time may come, however, when neither recognition nor resolution to respond differently can effect a change. We can get in over our heads and may need some real help to pull out. That help may come from a spouse, a friend, a counselor, from the resources of our faith, or better yet, from a combination of these.

We who are convinced that God Himself is the One who heals and makes us whole need to remain open to the different avenues through which He brings healing. He uses people, events, and the gifts of our own personality, by the power of His Spirit, to awaken insight within us and to move us in a creative direction. One mark of our rebellion against God is our unwillingness to receive help, or to receive help only if it comes packaged to our satisfaction. We may need to be reminded of what the Lord said: "This plan of mine is not what you would work out, neither are my thoughts the same as yours! For just as the heavens are higher than the earth, so are my ways higher than yours, and my thoughts than yours."[1]

The question then becomes, "Can I trust God?" Do we have any tangible reason for trusting Him? Yes! Jesus Christ's redemptive work gives us the clearest possible indication that we can trust our lives — past, present, and future — into His hands.

Part of trusting Him is trusting the life processes through which He takes us. Not that everything that happens to us is His perfect will, but He can operate within everything as we by faith open ourselves to Him. Opening myself to Christ in a given situation may mean opening myself to that person He has put in my life who can help me. He may use different people at different times to enable us to break through the walls that have been built around us by circumstances, by others, or by ourselves.

If your responses are becoming more uncontrollable — the tension building, conflict increasing, self-esteem diminishing; hostility, resentment, or self-pity piling up — it is time to take a personal inventory to try to find out what is pushing you out of control. Talking it out with an understanding, sympathetic person may be the most practical step to take. Gaining some objective insight into yourself at this point is absolutely essential.

Do not panic! A lot of people carry a deep fear of becoming mentally ill. Thinking that you are, and frantically trying to hide what you fear, can only propel you in a self-defeating direction. You may be going through a mild or even a serious emotional disturbance that can create much conflict within yourself and with others.

But remember, there is a way out of your dilemma. Many of the healthiest people I know have gained part of that health from struggling with emotional problems. Their awareness and sensitivity have been heightened both in the sense of what is going on in them and in what is happening to those around them.

I cannot prescribe an exercise or a process that will unlock all the doors of emotional distress. Throughout this section on handling personal conflicts are suggestions drawn from the positive resources of the Christian faith. However, insight alone may not be enough. Often we need someone who can help us appropriate the insight. God has given gifts to men, and some have the gift of *enabling and counseling.* They may not even be aware that their gifts of discernment and help come from God, but they can help nonetheless. No one need be embarrassed or ashamed to seek counsel. "The way of a fool is right in his own eyes: but he that hearkeneth unto counsel is wise."[2]

Read the Book of Proverbs (in the Old Testament) in one of the modern translations for some simple, practical suggestions that can help greatly in reorienting your life. To whet your appetite, let me share a few examples from the Living Bible:

> A relaxed attitude lengthens a man's life; jealousy rots it away. (14:30)
>
> Gentle words cause life and health; griping brings discouragement. (15:4)
>
> When a man is gloomy, everything seems to go wrong; when he is cheerful, everything seems right! (15:15)
>
> It is better to eat soup with someone you love than steak with someone you hate. (15:17)
>
> If you profit from constructive criticism you will be elected to the wise men's hall of fame. But to reject criticism is to harm yourself and your own best interests. (15:31,32)
>
> It is better to be slow-tempered than famous; it is better to have self-control than to control an army. (16:32)
>
> Any story sounds true until someone tells the other side and sets the record straight. (18:17)
>
> Steady plodding brings prosperity; hasty speculation brings poverty. (21:5)
>
> Being happy-go-lucky around a person whose heart is heavy is as

bad as stealing his jacket in cold weather, or rubbing salt in his wounds. (25:20)

A man who refuses to admit his mistakes can never be successful. But if he confesses and forsakes them, he gets another chance. (28:13)

In the end, people appreciate frankness more than flattery. (28:23)

Above all else, guard your affections. For they influence everything else in your life. (4:23)

Your own soul is nourished when you are kind; it is destroyed when you are cruel. (11:17)

Reverence for God gives a man deep strength; his children have a place of refuge and security. (14:26)

Sometimes our anxiety level may become so high that we cannot respond to verbal therapy alone. At this point we can be glad that medically there is a way to lessen our anxiety until we can recover sufficient strength to start moving in a constructive direction.

This brings me to a point of great concern. There seems to be a disparaging attitude in many camps today toward professional counselors. Part of this has been brought on by the counselors themselves. Some very inadequate approaches have been used and, as in every group, there are some charlatans around.

Another part of the problem is a movement today to deny that a real problem exists. Some simply write everything off as "sin." If you want to make your definition of sin broad enough to include every unhealthy thing present in the world — including moral rebellion, physical illness, and emotional distress — okay. But the biblical definition is narrower. Scripture says that sin is willful rebellion against God and transgression of His law; going one's own way, excluding the right of the Creator in one's life. It produces deliberate acts and attitudes of destruction and immorality and propagates selfishness, greed, and lust. Some make a distinction between the disease of sin (rebellion against God) and the symptoms of that disease (immorality, lying, brutality, etc.). Even so, the disease and its symptoms collaborate in destroying the person.

I believe a clear case can be made in both the Scripture and human experience that sin can, and often does, bring emotional illness and physical disease. *But not every emotional disturbance or physical illness is a direct result of personal sin.* Remember the story in the ninth chapter of John's Gospel of the man born blind? Christ's disciples assumed the man was blind either because of his own sin or his parents' sin. They asked, "'Master, . . . why was this man born blind? Was it a result of his own sins or those of his parents?' 'Neither,' Jesus answered."[3]

There was a fallacy in their theology, and the Lord used a concrete experience rather than a verbal presentation to correct their misconception.

In seeking out the root of the problem, one may discover that he has been living out his rebellion against God and God's moral laws. Should this be the case, repentance, confession, and responsible action could resolve the problem. If the individual has never invited the living Christ into his life to be his Savior and Lord, then this act of faith following his repentance could restore him to complete serenity.

If the emotional disturbance comes from stress that has gotten out of hand, or from an impairment of brain functions, or because a person's metabolism is out of balance, or he is carrying an overload of unresolved unconscious conflict, then the solution to his dilemma will be found in a different direction. Not away from faith, but faith in cooperation with the resources available within the realm of psychology, psychiatry, and medicine.

If I had acute appendicitis, I would not want a lay doctor to remove my appendix. If I felt uneasy about where I was emotionally and tried the suggested practical steps, yet my situation grew worse rather than better, I would look for some competent psychological or psychiatric help. Let me emphasize again that looking for competent professional help is not a denial of your faith or of the power of God in your life. It is one practical avenue through which God can touch us in a redemptive way even as He has used the medical profession in healing our physical ills.

Here are suggestions for those who may want to consult a competent counselor but do not know how to go about finding a reputable person in the field. If your church has a strong ministry in counseling with good results, you can start there. If you know someone who has had professional counseling with positive results, ask that person. If you have no personal contacts, you can check the resources available in your city or community. Look in the Yellow Pages of your telephone directory for "Counselors — Family Relations or Social Relations." When you call for an appointment, make sure the therapist is licensed and/or accredited by a legitimate accrediting agency, such as the American Psychiatric Association; the American Association of Marriage and Family Counselors; or the American Association of Pastoral Counselors. Ask where the therapist received his degree and what his specific field of study was. Find out how much experience the therapist has had, whom he uses for consultation, and what his fees are.

If you are satisfied with the answers you are given, proceed to make an appointment. If you are still uncertain, ask for the names of doctors, ministers, or others in the helping professions who refer clients to him. Thank the therapist or his secretary for the information, then call one or two of the persons named. Ask them if they can recommend a therapist to you and ask why they recommend the persons they do. This cross reference is quite legitimate and might give you a little more confidence in making a choice. By going through this simple process you will be increasing your odds greatly for finding competent help. During your first interview you can ask other questions that you feel will give you needed insight into the person you are trusting to help you through some hard places.

Finding qualified, competent help cannot be minimized when there is a personal, emotional, or social problem that you are unable to resolve or cope with adequately. Many illustrations could be given, but one suffices. When there is an emotional problem caused by a chemical imbalance within one's body, no amount of talk (religious, psychological, or otherwise) will relieve the distress. A competent counselor will be aware of this possibility and will want his client to get a thorough physical examination if the distress symptoms warrant it.

If the cost for therapy is beyond your means, check with the family service agencies and mental health agencies and/or counseling services provided by the churches in your city. Many of these agencies use a sliding scale fee: you pay according to your income. Regardless of your limitations, help is available.

Recognizing that we or someone close to us is in trouble emotionally is not automatic, nor is it easy. Most of the time, the behavioral changes will be gradual. Although we may notice some changes, they can come slowly enough to condition us to a new norm for ourselves or another. A friend of mine in another state has been reluctant to look for help even though he and his wife have been living in torment together. His wife is emotionally out of control; her emotional deterioration has come over a period of years, and during that time he has been conditioned to accepting his wife as a complaining, resentful person. He has not faced the fact that her behavior is abnormal. She is extremely paranoid — thinking everyone is out to get her. He has interpreted her actions as plain spite because she does not really love him. In reality she is expressing hostility toward him because he is not protecting her from her imagined enemies. How much misunderstanding and misery could have been avoided had either of them recognized what was developing years ago and taken some corrective measures!

Let me list some symptoms which, if they continue, suggest the possibility of loss of control. Like any other list of this nature, it is not all-inclusive. It usually takes a combination of factors and symptoms to push one beyond his limits. But to hedge against someone blindly struggling on without recognizing the situation, let us note some symptoms.

1. Insomnia, restlessness, and the loss of appetite.
2. Withdrawal from interpersonal relationships.
3. Sudden outbursts of rage with little or no provocation.
4. Long periods of depression.
5. Increased tendency to blame one's environment for his own shortcomings.
6. Excessive concern for conformity.
7. Oversensitivity to all types of stress.
8. Living with the feeling that something terrible is about to happen which has no rational basis in reality — extreme pessimism.
9. Personality disorganization — recognized in rapid mood changes, odd behavior, changes in sexual behavior with less interest or increased interest, changes in eating and sleeping patterns.
10. Persistent recurrence of distressing and sometimes horrifying thoughts.

11. Repetition of certain stereotyped acts.
12. Feelings of unreality and estrangement from oneself and his surroundings.
13. A persistent preoccupation with physical or emotional health.
14. State of being continually overwhelmed with feelings of worthlessness, guilt, and hopelessness.
15. Delusions and hallucinations.
16. Inappropriate responses to external circumstances.
17. Moving away from reality into a dream world.
18. Ambivalent feelings that tend to overwhelm and leave a person moody or depressed.
19. A flow of ideas that do not relate logically.
20. Absence of any drive or ambition; indifference; progressive vagueness.
21. Becoming overly jealous, suspicious, argumentative, and caustic.
22. Rapid mood swings, e.g., from elation to depression.
23. Becoming disoriented as to time, place, situation, or person.
24. Displaying inappropriate emotion, e.g., laughter when there should be tears.
25. Loss of emotional control, e.g., continuous crying.

For those who respond to suggestions excessively and feel that each statement describes you — *don't*. Every person can identify some of these symptoms within himself at different times. The important thing is not that you have once felt this way or that, or even that you do now. The important factors are (1) if the symptoms persist and increase; and (2) if they begin to disable you and impair normal functioning. Then you may need to seek out some competent help for working through these barriers to a fuller, freer experience of life and love.

There are disorders such as those of the psychopathic personality which must have intensive therapy. The psychopath has no conscience and seeks only immediate gratification. He has an extremely low frustration tolerance and either attacks the cause of frustration with intensity or flees without regard to the practical outcome of his action.

You cannot work through your differences with someone who is emotionally disturbed until the disturbance has been adequately resolved. There are no guarantees that a relationship will work when problems such as we have discussed are resolved. But we can be certain that the relationship does not have a chance until these problems are dealt with adequately.

Questions for Personal Reflection and Group Interaction

1. Have you ever personally known someone who became emotionally ill? What was your reaction? What would be your reaction should you encounter emotional illness?

2. Have you ever been afraid that you might be losing control? What did you do, or what would you do?

3. Have you ever lost control? What was it like? How did you regain control?

4. Is it hard for you to ask for help from another person? Why, or why not?

5. How would you describe your inner world to another? (Calm? uncertain? stormy?)

6. Do you ever have difficulty going to sleep? What kinds of things disturb your rest? Can you recognize a pattern?

7. Do you have someone with whom you can be totally open, or do you feel that you are really alone?

8. Which one of the statements from the Book of Proverbs included in this chapter speaks most clearly to where you are or want to be?

9. Are you aware of the resources available in your city or community for helping people deal with distressing problems and emotional disturbances?

10. Were you threatened by the list of symptoms included in this chapter? Why, or why not?

11. What are some positive things you can do to enhance the health of your own emotional life?

13. Single and Uncertain?

BEING SINGLE IN A couples' world can create many crises. Not the least of these is the feeling that it is a couples' world. Statistics lend pressure. If you are single and a female of twenty-one, you are a member of a minority group. If you are thirty-five, you are among 8 percent who have not been married. The male joins the minority group at twenty-three and at thirty-five finds that 86 percent of his age group are married.

Being single in a culture that is predominantly married can contribute enormously toward the development of a negative self-image. The feeling that there must be something wrong within both the single's mind and society's framework does not help an individual to grow or stimulate him to find and give his unique gift to the world.

From these negative feelings can come bitterness, depression, and the fear that one is missing life. This sometimes causes people to rush into unhealthy relationships or even marriage ill-prepared, simply because they want to escape their "disease" of singleness. Others may get hung up on the obsession that getting married would make everything beautiful. While I would never discourage anyone's dreams for companionship and intimacy, I must stress the reality that marriage does not solve all our problems. It may help solve some, but it also creates new ones. *The point is that "living" has to take place where we are, and not where we wish we were.*

We deal more specifically with the different kinds of crises which arise in divorce in the chapter "Living Beyond Our Failures." Here we will focus on attitudes and actions that can help the single person to live fully.

1. Marriage is not the only relationship that offers depth and intimacy. The single person can reach out to other singles, and couples as well, and develop significant friendships that will be mutually beneficial. One example on a large scale is the outreach of a ministry in Lubbock, Texas, called the Spiritual Growth Foundation. This fellowship of Christians has welcomed singles into its midst. Within their small groups literally hundreds of singles have found acceptance, support, and spiritual and social stimulation — in short, a family of people who care and about whom they can care. One cannot keep from being deeply moved by the loving, and sometimes confronting, community that is emerging in their company.

The Christian faith has within it the resources for including others as members of our spiritual family. These resources help us overcome our aloneness and feel that we too belong and have something of real value to contribute. Companionship is available outside marriage from friendships with both sexes.

Through the years a large number of singles have participated in our Bible studies, retreats, and small groups. Those with whom I have developed friendships have enriched my life and have helped me understand better the journey of authentic wholeness to which Christ calls us. The way can be lonely, but so it is with all of us at times, regardless of our marital or family status. However, those who feel the pain of the aloneness with the intensity that singleness brings can appreciate the gift of a caring friend in a way others miss.

2. Being single offers a unique freedom — the freedom of an unfettered life with opportunities to explore or move in almost any area or direction you choose. An old proverb says, He who travels lightest, travels farthest. As a single person you can make this proverb true for yourself. Your life can be lived in greater simplicity with freer movement. The creative possibilities for investing yourself are almost limitless. But for your creativity to be released you must accept yourself and your singleness as a gift to be given to others, and not as a curse. Paul's statement relating to whether one should marry or remain single summarizes the point well: "But be sure in deciding these matters that you are living as God intended, marrying or not marrying in accordance with God's direction and help, and accepting whatever situation God has put you into."[1]

3. Being single today does not necessarily mean that your singleness is permanent. The same is also true if you are married: illness, death, or divorce could alter your situation quickly.

Just because you are thirty and single is no reason to shut your life to the possibility of marriage. Many do. They begin to withdraw and enter into cycles of depression, because they fear that there must be something wrong with them or that God is cruelly allowing life to pass them by.

The secret is to live life as fully as possible *now* instead of fretting over either the past (what might have been) or the future (what may not be). I know it is much easier said than done, but so is everything worthwhile in life.

4. Christ can make your singleness a gift. He can increase your sensitivity to people who hurt and feel unfulfilled. He can flow His love into desolate places through you and can bless others as they identify with your singleness and begin to share in the hope your faith brings.

I had a professor in college, Dr. McChristi, who lost her fiancé in World War I. She never married. But she gave herself so completely and so unselfishly to her students that her singleness became a gift of love to all of us. She taught English — never my favorite subject — but in her class I learned more about life and authentic Christianity, as well as English, than in any other single course I ever had.

5. Remember, too, that Christ Himself was single. He gave Himself to all of us that we might be able to give to one another. He was truly human! He understands your feelings and your needs, and He can enable you to make the most of your singleness if you let Him.

6. Christ does not come to displace any other person in our lives. He comes to take His rightful place as God, but this by no means squeezes out the need for human love. We were made to live in fellowship with God and with each other. To have a right relationship to God means that we are only partially fulfilled. This is the way God made us. But fulfillment on the human level may or may not come in marriage. As we have already discussed, the need for human love and companionship may have to be met in small doses by different friends and by Christian brothers and sisters. There may not be that one person with whom we can share our whole self for the rest of our lives.

Sex — asset or liability — is brought into full focus when we face our singleness. The need for intimacy spiritually, emotionally, and physically is part of our God-given nature. Like all the other great gifts of being, sex can bless if used correctly and can curse if used selfishly. We cannot separate the self from sexuality. Part of being is either masculine or feminine. To color each the same is to impoverish life, stifle creativity, and make a mockery of God's wisdom.

The Judeo-Christian pattern for sexual expression and control, as found in the Bible, still offers the best guidelines we have. Walter Trobisch in his book *I Loved a Girl* answers a letter that a young man wrote to him with regard to a sex experience outside marriage. Here are some concrete answers that are biblically based and emotionally sound:

My dear Francois,

Let us put aside for a moment the question of whether or not your case should be called adultery. You are absolutely right in saying that sex is no sin. Your desires, your thoughts when seeing a beautiful girl are not yet sin; neither is it sin if you feel attracted. You can't avoid physical desires any more than you can avoid having the birds fly around your head. But you can certainly prevent them from building nests in your hair.

√ Indeed, sexual desires are created by God. They are a gift of God, one of the most precious gifts you have received for your young life. But the existence of a desire does not justify its satisfaction. The presence of a power does not imply that one should be guided by it, blindly and without restraint. . . .

[Sex] should be used, but in its proper place and time, according to God's plan. Within that plan the sexual instinct is a good thing, a powerful source of life and unity between two beings. Outside of God's plan, it quickly becomes a means of division, a source of cruelty, perversion and death.

√ I could say it also this way: Within God's will, sexual union fulfills its purpose only when it is an expression of love.

One phrase in your letter struck me especially. You wrote, "I loved a girl." No, my friend. You did not love that girl; you went to bed with her — these are two completely different things. You had a sexual episode, but what love is, you did not experience. . . . for love wants to *give*. Love seeks to make the other one happy, and not himself. You acted like a pure egoist. Instead of saying: "I loved a girl," you should have said: "I loved myself and myself only. For this purpose I misused a girl." . . .

√ No, you did not love her. True love involves responsibility — the one for the other and both before God. Where love is, you no longer say, "I," but "you"; "I am responsible for you. You are responsible for me." Together then you stand before God where you do not say "you and I," but rather "we."

√ Only in marriage does this "we" become a full reality. Only in marriage can love really unfold and mature, because only there can it find permanence and faithfulness. True love never can and never will end. That's why you should use the great words, "I love you" very sparingly. You should save it for the girl whom you intend to marry.

√ Here in marriage is the right place to use your sexual powers. There they will help you to love your wife. They are one expression — one among many others — by means of which you make her understand how much you love her.

If you use your sexual powers apart from this kind of love, you are preparing yourself for an unhappy marriage. . . .

Sincerely yours,[2]
T.

Then from a woman's perspective, listen to Gini Andrews in her book, *Your Half of the Apple:*

Don't put yourself in situations where your hormones get in such an uproar that you can't hear anything, let alone the quiet voice of God, and then say, "Why has He made me this way?" He made you a physical being, a marvelous, responsive being called Woman, but, like the rest of His Creation, you are involved in the laws that govern His universe. As you don't expect to bring a magnet up to steel shavings and have the shavings back off, don't expect to put yourself in a situation where the magnetism and power of sex become total and then pray like mad or blame God for putting you together as He has![3]

Within human nature there is the feeling that we are exceptions. Things work one way for everyone else, but we think we can make things work for us any way we choose. There are no exceptions to God's moral law. We need to face this squarely and decide ahead of time what standard we will adhere to in the matter of dating and sex. I have listened to the heartache of too many people who tried other ways and failed miserably to feel any need to be less than candid in this matter.

For those who have made mistakes in sexual conduct, the good news of the gospel is that there is forgiveness and healing in Christ. Christ forgave the woman in adultery and said to her, "Go, and sin no more."[4] He was tender with those who failed in this matter, but He never lowered the standard for any.

What can the single person do with the sexual energy and drive inherent in being male or female? Pour it into a creative, constructive direction. Great music, poetry, art, and literature have often come from those who, not being able to give themselves to an individual in marriage, gave themselves to humanity instead. The apostle Paul is but one example.

Let's also face the fact that complete fulfillment of one's sexual needs cannot occur outside a tender, growing marriage. Paul advised in his first letter to the Corinthians that if the frustration is more than you can bear, pray for a wife or husband who can meet your needs as a total person and you, theirs. Work at being the right person. Allow some friendships to ripen with the opposite sex without making the possibility of marriage uppermost in your mind.

Remember, God knows you are single. He loves you and will use you where you are. Every person is of great value to Him —

your marital status does not increase or decrease your worth in His family, nor in His economy. *Amen!*

Questions for Personal Reflection and Group Interaction

1. How do you feel about being single, if you are? If you are married, how do you feel about those who are not married?
2. Do you have any relationships that offer depth and intimacy?
3. Do you feel that you really do have something of worth to give to others?
4. Do you see your singleness as a gift, or as a curse?
5. Do you ever get caught up in *fretting* over the past (what might have been) or over the future (what may not be)?
6. What has helped you to make the most of your present situation?
7. Have you ever given God thanks for the gift of your sexuality?
8. If God would grant you three wishes, what would you ask for? Why?

14. Conflict Between Parents and Adolescents

IT'S NOT EASY BEING a teen-ager, and it's even harder parenting one properly. The reasons for this situation are legion. The adolescent is undergoing many changes physically, emotionally, socially, and intellectually. He is being inwardly propelled away from his dependent role toward a more independent one. He must assert himself more as he finds himself to be a distinct person rather than an extension of his parents. The opinions of his peers seem more important than the wishes of his parents. Concepts, values, and traditions which he never questioned before must now undergo real scrutiny. Maturity demands that he move beyond "what I've been told" to "what I believe." To compound the problem even more, most adolescents feel inadequate. Being no longer a child but not yet an adult is an awkward place to be.

A struggling teen-ager has moved beyond the childhood stage, but is still dependent on his parents for finances, home, and more. He has the growing need to become his own man and order his own life, which is a beautiful sign of budding maturity. Part of being

126

his own person, however, is assuming the responsibilities inherent in that position — namely, providing for his own needs and perhaps the needs of others as well. He may take some reassurance from the fact that the awkward place in which he now finds himself is only temporary. This, of course, could be good news to your parents as well. *There is one attitude which we all must guard against — insisting on freedom or independence without accepting the responsibilities demanded by such freedom.* One without the other leads to a greater dependency and blocks the flow of creative growth.

Adolescence is an exciting and important time in a person's life. It can be the best he has ever experienced, or it can be a disaster. The teen-ager himself, more than anyone else, determines which it will be.

The adolescent must listen to the adults who play significant roles in his life. They are imperfect. They have made mistakes, but they also have experience which can prove invaluable on the journey into adulthood.

The teen years are an excellent time to discover that God is not an extension of one's parents or of the current hero. God broke into history two thousand years ago in Jesus Christ to let us know what He is like and how much He cares for us. He wants you to discover that you are "a unique, unrepeatable miracle of God." There has never been another person exactly like you, and there never will be. God has a special purpose for your life. What it is, you must discover.

The place to start is to read the record of God's entry into history to find out who He is and what He wants to do in your life. Read the Gospel of John in a modern translation with this question in mind: "What is God really like?" As He confronts you with His great love, pray and ask the living Christ to come into your life and forgive you for all the selfish things you've done and begin to make you into the beautiful person He has dreamed of your becoming. This will begin the most significant adventure of your entire life — your walk with God! He will help you turn problems into opportunities for growth, weaknesses into strength, and failures into success. You will still make mistakes, but you can recover from them. Your life can enrich whatever part of the world you touch. What God longs to do in you is so great that it would stagger your imagination and leave you speechless if you only knew! Go find His dream for you, if you really want to ride the high waves.

Parenting an adolescent has its problems too. Attempting to give them more freedom with its concomitant responsibility; permitting them to question the values which give your life meaning, while helping them understand the necessity of adequate values; allowing room for their current fads; exerting authority over them without provoking them to anger; showing warmth and sympathy without "babying" them; exercising discipline without rejection, direction without domination, flexibility without indecisiveness — all this can humble the wisest and exhaust the most creative. *Accepting this time in the life of your son or daughter as the adventure it is instead of fearing it, is the first step toward the kind of attitude that will enable you to cope with the challenge at hand.* Learn to grow with your teen-ager, for the Lord will use the joy and the pain to stretch you and to teach you more fully the essence of love.

When conflicts come, which they will, here are some suggestions for both the parent and the adolescent that can help make the dissension creative and not destructive.

1. Each must accept the other as a growing person. None of us have arrived, and we all make mistakes. Instead of allowing this reality to threaten us and make us defensive, it can enable us to be more understanding of the other's struggle — whether it be the adolescent trying his ways and failing miserably, or the parent who at the moment is having a hard time coping with the son's or daughter's erratic life-style.

2. Work at keeping an open, honest relationship. Stop playing games or manipulating each other. When you don't understand, say so. Express your true feeling, but in the context of a genuine desire to understand where the other person is.

3. Make sure your conversations do not become monologues. Listen to one another. Talk to each other. You will know that the relationship is moving where it should when you can laugh and cry, if need be, with one another.

I have a friend in Richmond, Indiana, who really worked at keeping an honest dialogue going with his daughter. She fell for a guy who had no motivation or direction for his life: he was an adult hippie. My friend did not throw a fit or raise a big fuss. He took his daughter to dinner one evening, as he had been doing periodically through the years, and they simply talked about the situation. The daughter backed away from her relationship with the young man, not because her father insisted she do so, but because she came to see that he could not fulfill her, nor she him, given their differences.

4. Parents must not abnegate their role in the face of conflict. Many parents act as though they are afraid of their children. It is true that our children know us well enough to expose our weaknesses and to attack us where it hurts. But that is part of being human. The best are weak, so we need not waste energy being defensive about our frailty. As parents, we must exercise our authority in saying yes or no and in establishing proper boundaries and guidelines. The adolescent wants and needs fences, but may revolt against them anyway. Tough love may have to be exercised, but exercised wisely.

5. The parents need to make sure that the adolescent knows they are for him. By listening, talking openly, and reassuring him in words and deeds that you care, you are sending the positive message of *being for him* even if you are having to say no to what he wants at the moment. Of course, if you are too busy in your own activities to pay serious attention to your adolescent's needs, then you are sending an "I don't care" message loud and clear. Reconciliation can come only when this message is changed both verbally and nonverbally to read, "I care very deeply about you and your needs."

6. It is essential that parents seek the best for their children and at the same time resist trying to live their lives over in them. Our children are unique persons in their own right. We have them for a brief time to love, discipline, and teach, and then we must release them for their own pilgrimage in the larger community of society. To see them grow into maturity and take their places in the world as productive people makes you rich indeed and will give you cause to celebrate God's gift to you the rest of your days. Your investment in your children is perhaps the most significant investment of your life.

7. Give your emerging adult more and more room to grow and become his own person. A gradual turning loose is much better than a sudden one. Work at helping him accept the responsibilities of

his increased freedom. This will even help him understand you better.

If would be helpful if your adolescent would read this chapter and then use it as a springboard for the two of you to talk about where you are in your relationship. Following are some basic principles for the adolescent to give thought to:

1. The God who knows best the essentials for life calls you to "obey your parents; this is the right thing to do because He has placed them in authority over you. Honor your father and mother. This is the first of God's Ten Commandments that ends with a promise. And this is the promise: that if you honor your father and mother, yours will be a long life, full of blessing."[1] Maintaining a healthy relationship with your parents by learning how to submit to their proper authority will equip you for real life in more ways than you can imagine. It's difficult at times to do so, because you see your parents' mistakes and because you, like everyone else, would really like to have your own way. But as we learn to bend our wills to our parents', it becomes easier to submit our wills to God. And it is in submitting to God that we experience the kind of authentic freedom we all seek.

2. You honor your parents when you see them as persons rather than as bank accounts or disciplinarians or someone to try to outmaneuver. Parents have feelings, too. They need acceptance and understanding, just as you do. Try looking at them as real people, and see if you do not get excited about living and growing with them.

3. You honor your parents by passing on to others in your life now (and to those who will be a part of your life in the future) the love they have given you. You will probably have a teen-aged son or daughter some day, and conflict will begin again — only this time you will be the parent and someone else will be the adolescent. How would you like that relationship to be? Work at making yours that way now with your parents.

The most satisfying course is for the parents and the adolescent to be deeply committed Christians who will pray together that God would help them make their family a shining witness in a dark world.

Questions for Personal Reflection
and Group Interaction

1. Do you recognize the glory and the agony inherent in the growing process?
2. Is — or was — growing up hard for you? Why? In what ways?
3. Has your growing up been hard on your parents? Why?
4. As a parent, what has been the hardest thing for you in parenting your children? What positive insights have come out of your parenting role? If you had it to do all over, what changes would you make? Can you make that insight a gift to others who are in the parenting process?
5. Have you come to any new insights about yourself, your children, your parents, or the life process from this chapter? What? Is there something you need to work on?

15. Conflict With Parents and In-Laws

A COMMON AND PAINFUL crisis that most, if not all, married couples face comes either from the earlier failure to establish a healthy relationship with their parents or from the deterioration of that relationship. It's not easy for parents to turn their children loose. They want the best for them and, after spending years playing a protective role, it only seems natural to hold on regardless of age or maturity.

Wise parents recognize this tendency and take steps to assure that the apron strings are cut at the proper time. But sometimes parents fail to realize that they are meddling beyond their rightful boundaries. When parents display the desire to "own their own," you can rest assured that a negative relationship will emerge. The feeling arises that no one is good enough for their son or daughter, or that the in-law is failing to take proper care of their offspring.[1] This attitude usually grows out of parental resentment of another's taking their place as number one in their son's or daughter's affection. Bitterness can grow and become vicious in extreme cases.

The other aspect of this is that a son-in-law or daughter-in-law may be jealous of his spouse's parents and may attempt to destroy all filial affection for them. This attitude usually comes from a deep insecurity that causes the person having it to feel threatened by everyone who holds a place of esteem in the spouse's eyes. Should this be the case, deliberate steps should be taken to deal with the root cause.

If this jealousy seems to be your problem, ask yourself, "Why am I so insecure that I cannot share my spouse's affections with his or her parents? Does loving them diminish his or her love for me?" If it genuinely seems to do so, perhaps the apron string needs to be cut more completely. If not, ask the living Christ to help you relax inside and to become generous with your in-laws. Ask Him to help you see them as persons who are part of you now, and not as competitors for your spouse's affection. Take the risk of talking openly and frankly about your feelings and your struggle here with your spouse. This will give him the opportunity to clear up misunderstandings and to examine his own attitudes and reactions toward both you and his parents. Remember, it's never too late to start sharing openly and frankly with your spouse.

If a parent is interfering, then the son or daughter of that parent must take a firm stand. Do not leave it to your spouse to go against your parents. You must do it with your spouse's support and understanding. *To be healthy, the relationship between parents, adult offspring, and in-laws must be a peer relationship and not a parent-child one.* The parents as well as the son or daughter need to work at relating on the peer level. Should either refuse, there is but one way in which the marriage will be enabled to grow — pull away from the parents sufficiently to allow the breaking of the old patterns. In time, make a concerted effort to establish a healthy relationship. You say it's painful to rupture a lifetime attachment. Yes, it is! But it's more painful not to do it, if you want your marriage to succeed.

Remember the first principle God gave us for establishing a home: "Therefore shall a man leave his father and his mother, and shall cleave unto his wife: and they shall be one flesh."[2] In reality it is this *leaving* and *cleaving* that opens the way for both a new family to emerge and new relationships with parents to unfold.

*Questions for Personal Reflection
and Group Interaction*

1. Has it been difficult for you to cut the apron strings? Why?
2. Have you ever been jealous of your spouse's affection toward his/her parents? How have you handled the situation? Do you need to handle it differently?
3. Can you share openly and deeply with your spouse? Why not? What were your parent models like in the matter of sharing? Did they communicate easily?
4. Do you have a *peer* relationship with your parents and in-laws and/or your adult children and their spouses? If not, how can you best go about enabling such a relationship to emerge?

16. Living Beyond Our Failures

TRY AS WE MAY, EVERY one of us will experience failure in some relationship. There may be a rift between friends, business associates, employers and employees, or within the family structure with divorce, parent-child conflict, or in-law clashes. We need to realize that the more intimate the relationship, the more painful the failure. The loss of a distant friend may bring regrets, but the loss of a spouse may create a devastating trauma that seriously threatens our sanity.

A commitment on our part to make a relationship work helps greatly, but does not guarantee that it will endure. It takes both persons involved to make any relationship succeed. One cannot give to the other indefinitely. If either person decides to terminate the relationship and refuses to be persuaded otherwise, the end is inevitable. The problem is that it's not always clear just when the line has been crossed and the relationship ceases to hold any future potential.

Divorce is one of the more clear-cut relational breaks, identified not only by the evident hurt but also by the laws of the land.

You were married, now you are divorced: that is a distinct signal which indicates that, apart from some miraculous intervention, the relationship is nil and it is useless to continue investing energy in its recovery.

Divorce brings with it potential for a wide variety of new crises.

1. Divorce creates an identity crisis. One moves from being part of a couple to being single. The new position and role demand identity alteration.

2. Divorce may create a security crisis. Divorced persons may be forced to depend more on themselves and may experience tremendous uncertainty about their new position in life.

3. Divorce may create an economic crisis. The need for the wife to support herself and perhaps her children, or the husband's having to support himself plus the family he has lost, can be an extremely heavy financial load. The necessity of managing the resources one does have may be new and difficult.

4. Divorce creates a social crisis. The familiar circle of friends and acquaintances may no longer be comfortable. For many, making new friends is not easy.

5. Divorce creates "parenting" problems for both the wife and the husband. The parent who has custody of the children has the stretching task, as a single parent, of creating an atmosphere of security that engenders stability and a sense of well-being. The absent parent will have to struggle not to communicate rejection by that absence.

6. Divorce may create traumatic conflict for the children. They have the need to love both parents and to be loved by both. Therefore the separation of the two most important people in their world will affect them deeply.

7. Divorce may create a religious crisis. This can be healthy. We can be grateful that under the stress of separation and divorce many people turn to God for help. But the Christian community has not always known what to do with people in this situation. The divorced are not always welcome — for several reasons. One is that the church has not always known how to uphold the *ideal* of marriage for life and, at the same time, minister

to those who have failed in this regard. The divorced can be a threat simply because others do not understand and do not know what to say or how to help.

Divorced persons themselves may question where they stand in relation to what they have been taught, and they may not feel free to move back into the Christian community. But the church is intended to be a vital medium through which God expresses His love for all men, broken as we are!

It must be emphasized that to fail in a particular aspect of one's life, such as marriage, does not mean you are a failure as a person. You are not a failure! You failed at being married,

After we have done everything we possibly can to restore a disintegrating relationship without success, we must then move ahead, for contrary to the negative feelings of the moment, *there is much good yet to experience both within ourselves and within the context of old and new relationships.* We need to remember that God's love and grace are sufficient to see us through these failures and enable us to live again. He does not erase the pain or the memory, but He will take us through a healing process as we give Him permission to do so.

God's healing process can change a potentially crippling experience into a redemptive asset for living life deeply and meaningfully.

1. In the midst of our conflict and failure, Christ can enable us to face ourselves more realistically than perhaps we ever would if left to the comfort and safety of our own undisturbed existence. The potential for redemptive meaning is always present in our failure.

I have counseled a man who has in the past been unwilling to face himself or admit his weaknesses, which have been painfully noticeable to his wife. He has criticized and belittled his wife for seventeen years. The reason for his action is that he hates women. During his formative years his mother had a series of affairs — leaving him and his dad sometimes for weeks. The result is a deep distrust and lack of respect for women. He shared with me that he had been vaguely aware of these feelings, but when his wife left him, they surfaced. The progress he made in the next two months opened the possibility for reestablishing himself with his wife. Hopefully they will make it.

It seems true that most of us allow significant changes to occur only when we are forced by pressure we cannot avoid.

2. The living Christ can use our struggle to make us less critical and more sensitive to others who struggle. The Spiritual Growth Foundation in Lubbock, Texas, which I mentioned in an earlier chapter, has pioneered in many respects an outreach to singles, the divorced, and parents without partners. The acceptance within these groups and the caring they show one another are remarkable. They know what it's like; they have been there, and many of them are still there. But they are being Christ's people to each other and are lessening the loneliness and lightening the load. Their ability to identify is a gift of their own suffering.

3. Christ can restore our sense of a *future with promise*. Conflict and failure often lead to depression, and depression leaves one with the feeling that he has no future — nothing to look forward to or to celebrate. This futility can be so devastating as to lead to suicide. Because of Christ's sufferings, however, we have a future now and forever. You may *feel* that everything has come to an end, but the *fact* is, there is more to experience, to discover, to celebrate, and to share. Open yourself to receive the life that is promised.

Let your failure be the occasion for making a leap of faith toward Christ. Being down and defeated is an opportune time to look up. Acknowledge your mistakes and rebellion to Him, and ask Him to come into your life to do what He dreams and purposes for you. The Scriptures declare of Christ that "he was in the world, and the world was made by him, and the world knew him not. He came unto his own, and his own received him not. But as many as received him, to them gave he power to become the sons of God, even to them that believe on his name."[1]

Ask God's forgiveness for the mistakes you made which contributed to failures in a relationship. As evidence that you are receiving His forgiveness, forgive yourself. Without a genuine sense of forgiveness, we can never be free.

Ask Christ to help you be responsible in your situation. Often, when we are down, there is a great temptation to continue in a downward spiral. To succumb is to open ourselves to more hurt; to withdraw blocks the possibility of new, creative relationships. An irresponsible or insensitive attitude can keep us from recognizing the depth of the relationships we still have and from enjoying the richness they offer.

Give yourself permission to deal with your negative feelings, but not to wallow in them. Hurt and grief come in every failure — but so does hope. The Good News means that we can live through anything except our refusal to live through it. The first major step is deciding that you want to recover. This decision will give you sufficient motivation for seeking the kind of answers that will create authentic freedom.

Look for Christian fellowship. We need each other. Part of belonging to Christ is belonging to His people. Many times the people who come to me for counseling minister to me more profoundly than they will ever know. It is always a two-way experience.

We are all strugglers in some fashion. As we share with each other, the struggle becomes easier and Christian community becomes a redemptive reality. You are neither the first nor the last person who has failed. Hopefully your struggle will help you realize your kinship with the rest of humanity.

Finally, do not hesitate to reach out to others who may be hurting. This enables us to move beyond the self-pity stage and begin rebuilding our own sense of worth. To sit and look at our own problems only causes them to increase. To reach beyond ourselves to make another's way easier contributes enormously to our own release.

Several years ago the truth of this concept was brought home to me dramatically in the fellowship of the Church of the Saviour in Washington, D.C. A man of twenty-seven had been under psychiatric care for ten years. Yet, with all this help, he still had been unable to function well enough to hold a job. The night we met him, he was helping an alcoholic. His concern for the man was genuine, and he was obviously excited. Some of the group members shared with us after he left that they were encouraged about the progress he was making. He had a job and was functioning well in it.

This man's recovery had been impeded, in part, by those

who had tried to help. For ten years everyone around him focused on his problems, and he did the same. It was not until he focused on another's problem and tried to help that he began to recover. Christ said, "Whoever clings to his life shall lose it, and whoever loses his life shall save it."[2] Invest yourself in helping others find their way, and you will find that His way will open to you.

Christ specializes in enabling us to live beyond our failures!

Questions for Personal Reflection and Group Interaction

1. Are you experiencing at present, or have you experienced in the past, a failure in some significant relationship which is causing or has caused great concern and pain for you? How are you handling the situation, or how did you handle it?
2. If you are divorced, which crises listed in this chapter seem the most painful to you at present?
3. Can you make a distinction for yourself between having failed in one aspect of your life, such as marriage, and being a failure as a person? The former does not include the latter.
4. What constructive things can you recognize as having come from a relationship failure?
5. How can you use your failures redemptively?
6. What are some practical steps you can take to aid the recovery process?

PART THREE

Coping With Tough
Circumstances

We are pressed on every side by troubles, but not crushed and broken. We are perplexed because we don't know why things happen as they do, but we don't give up and quit. We are hunted down, but God never abandons us. We get knocked down, but we get up again and keep going. These bodies of ours are constantly facing death just as Jesus did; so it is clear to all that it is only the living Christ within [who keeps us safe].

—2 Corinthians 4:8-10
The Living Bible

amen + amen

17. Where Did It All Begin?

SINCE THE BEGINNING of history, man has sought to escape the pain inherent in his existence and to control his circumstances to guarantee for himself what he considers to be life's best. Adam in the Garden of Eden rebelled against the limits placed upon him, not by a tyrant, but by a loving Creator who gave him everything except the fruit of one tree. He was not satisfied to be himself — a magnificent creature made in the image of the infinite God with dominion over all the earth. Adam wanted to be as God — totally in charge of himself and his world, independent of God. The same desire persists today in the human heart.

Thus began the upheaval and distress so prevalent in the human story. Theologians refer to this event as the Fall, and its repercussions are felt throughout God's created order. This simple yet profound revelation of God can set the stage for understanding human nature and the tragedies of life.

This world does not offer a painless, carefree existence. Both good and evil are present. Nature herself has imbalances that contribute disaster from wind and rain, drought and disease. There are birth defects and human disabilities of all kinds. One man's description is apropos: "How frail is man, how few his days, how full of trouble! He blossoms for a moment like a flower — and withers; as the shadow of a passing cloud, he quickly disappears."[1] Few if any will live long without severe adversity of some kind. Life will bring many events into our experience over which we have no control. Still, our freedom is not totally obliterated, for we can choose the way we attempt to cope with the things that overwhelm us. In the midst of the struggle, we can affirm that this is a fit place for personality to grow and for people to become great as they discover the reality of God's love and grace in their lives.

God takes man and his choices seriously and, as we have pointed out, guarantees a significant degree of freedom to him. What we do, say, think, and feel carries tremendous consequences for good or ill, not only for ourselves, but for everyone we touch. Eventually our touch encompasses the world. The good or evil we do becomes a part of the history and heritage of the whole human race. It does not die or disappear with us. If we indulge in immorality, dishonesty, deceit, hate, bigotry, or greed, we contribute to the spiritual blindness of mankind and push the race further toward the darkness. If we rape the land, pollute the air and the water, we give the world hunger and disease. Other people's mistakes affect us even as ours affect them. God does not stop the life process every thirty minutes to reverse the consequences of men's deeds. We have to cope with the fruit of our folly as well as share the goodness of responsible action.

Our names may be forgotten by men, but our influence will be felt for eternity. This means that living has much greater significance than our mere enjoyment of temporal pleasures. There is a drama unfolding in God's economy which allows us to be participants in a redemptive endeavor so great that not even God can exhaust it in eternity.[2] Such a statement will be only words to those who are not hungry for meaning beyond themselves and their own pleasures. But for those who yearn to find their true identity and to discover the reason for their existence, it can stir the heart and fire the imagination. You are called to be the sons of God by faith in Christ, and as sons you will share in all God has for His dear children!

A *position of faith in Christ does not make us immune* to *suffering*. It will include suffering. "And since we are his children, we will share his treasures — for all God gives to his Son Jesus is now ours too. But if we are to share his glory, we must also share his suffering."[3]

Another characteristic of human nature is to seek the easy way, avoiding discipline and uncomfortable demands if possible. But a diamond did not become a diamond by lying in a comfortable position. Diamonds are crystals of pure carbon that have been exposed to tremendous pressure and heat. Were the carbon animate, it probably would not understand the pressure being exerted upon it. It would undoubtedly question the wisdom behind the process — "Why is this happening to me? Is there any purpose for my suffering? How could God or anyone allow such things to occur?" Being made into a diamond would hurt! In fact, at times it would seem that one was being totally destroyed. At those times, even if the carbon were informed that it was being transformed into a diamond, it would respond, "I don't want to be a diamond; it's not worth it!" But out of seeming destruction comes a beautiful creation which will enrich the world and in which the diamond itself shall ultimately rejoice and affirm that it has been worth it all.

Listen to the witness of a man who found the secret that enabled him to make the most of his tough circumstances:

> So now, since we have been made right in God's sight by faith in his promises, we can have real peace with him because of what Jesus Christ our Lord has done for us. For because of our faith, he has brought us into this place of highest privilege where we now stand, and we confidently and joyfully look forward to actually becoming all that God has had in mind for us to be. We can rejoice, too, when we run into problems and trials for we know that they are good for us — they help us learn to be patient. And patience develops strength of character in us and helps us trust God more each time we use it until finally our hope and faith are strong and steady. Then, when that happens, we are able to hold our heads high no matter what happens and know that all is well, for we know how dearly God loves us. . . .[4]

These words did not come from a man who never felt pain, rejection, or fear for his life or for the life of another. In telling his story he said,

> Five different times the Jews gave me their terrible thirty-nine lashes. Three times I was beaten with rods. Once I was stoned.

Three times I was shipwrecked. Once I was in the open sea all night and the whole next day. I have traveled many weary miles and have been often in great danger from flooded rivers, and from robbers, and from my own people, the Jews, as well as from the hands of the Gentiles. I have faced grave dangers from mobs in the cities and from death in the deserts and in the stormy seas and from men who claim to be brothers in Christ but are not. I have lived with weariness and pain and sleepless nights. Often I have been hungry and thirsty and have gone without food; often I have shivered with cold, without enough clothing to keep me warm.

Then, besides all this, I have the constant worry of how the churches are getting along: Who makes a mistake and I do not feel his sadness? Who falls without my longing to help him? Who is spiritually hurt without my fury rising against the one who hurt him?[5]

Yet, in the midst of his struggle and with the load he carried, Paul discovered that the resources of his faith were sufficient not only to enable survival, but to make his life an adventure.

To discover those resources for ourselves is the objective of this section of the book.

Questions for Personal Reflection
and Group Interaction

1. Can you identify the ways you attempt to control your world? Does it always work?
2. Have you ever felt that the world is a cruel place in which to live? What brought on such feelings?
3. Have you ever faced the reality of how much your actions and attitudes affect other people?
4. On a scale from 0 to 10, which number would best represent your *sense of significance* as a person? How important do you believe you are to others?
5. What gives your life meaning? What is that meaning?
6. What resources have you discovered that have enabled you to survive the tough places better?

18. No One Is Exempt

THE WAY MOST PEOPLE feel about tragedy is that "it happens to others, but it will not happen to me." We can be grateful that of the multitude of things which could go wrong, only a very small percentage actually occurs. That fraction can overwhelm us, however, even if we are prepared for it.

I do not intend to frighten anyone or create needless anxiety, but to help us realistically accept the boundaries of our humanity. If we make the mistake of believing that life for us here will always continue as is, we may not ask the questions that can lead us in the direction of finding meaning that reaches beyond our years and will enable us to survive the hard places. Let's face this fact: unless the Lord returns in our lifetime, none of us is going to get out of this world alive.

Life never remains stationary. We are always going through changes — some we can readily affirm and some we may fear or dread. As much as we want to, we cannot make the difficulties go away and never return.

Although we never thought it would happen to us, when it does we tend to feel that we are the only ones to whom it has happened. In our crisis we experience great loneliness. We may feel estranged from everyone. Those not caught in our struggle and hurt seem distant and unreal to us. The temptation will be to allow self-pity to rule. Yet reality reveals that we are not the first to suffer great pain or loss, and neither will we be the last.

Another part of the problem is focused for us by the struggle of the author of Psalm 73, in contrast with a statement made by the writer of Proverbs. Proverbs declares, "The way of transgressors is hard."[1] And so it is. There are times, however, when it seems not to be so, as the writer of Psalm 73 expressed:

> As for me, I came so close to the edge of the cliff! My feet were slipping and I was almost gone. For I was envious of the prosperity of the proud and wicked. Yes, all through life their road is smooth! They grow sleek and fat. They aren't always in trouble and plagued with problems like everyone else. . . . These fat cats have everything their hearts could ever wish for! They scoff at God and threaten his people. . . . Have I been wasting my time? Why take the trouble to be pure? All I get out of it is trouble and woe — every day and all day long! . . . It is so hard to explain it — this prosperity of those who hate the Lord.[2]

But as he reflected on the situation, when he was not hurting so deeply, the psalmist saw the truth more clearly.

> What a slippery path they are on — suddenly God will send them sliding over the edge of the cliff and down to their destruction: an instant end to all their happiness, an eternity of terror. Their present life is only a dream! They will awaken to the truth as one awakens from a dream of things that never really were![3]

The answer to the problem of why the wicked prosper and the righteous suffer finds no solution if limited to this world, but if examined in the context of eternity the answer becomes clear. The Scriptures say that "if being a Christian is of value to us only now in this life, we are the most miserable of creatures."[4] The Christian faith addresses itself to the whole of life and to the entire range of man's existence. It speaks meaningfully about life in the present, but always includes the future. Christians are pilgrims discovering who they are as the people of God and how they can live purposefully in this world with a sense of destiny for the future. We are on our way to something so great that "the sufferings of this present time are not worth comparing with the glory that is to be revealed to us."[5] It is not pie in the sky by and by.

God's activity in human life is so magnificent that it will take two worlds for it to be unfolded: this one with its joys and sorrows, successes and failures; and eternity where all hindrances, pain, and struggle will be absent. The Christian faith neglects neither our past, affirming our assets and offering forgiveness and the power to change our weaknesses; our present, with resources for experiencing life as an adventure; nor our future, with the promise that "eye hath not seen, nor ear heard, neither have entered into the heart of man, the things which God hath prepared for them that love him."[6] It does make a difference whether we serve ourselves or the Lord — an incredible difference!

God brings good into every person's life, believer and nonbeliever alike. "But whatever is good and perfect comes to us from God."[7] Life itself, personality, autonomy, and the capacity to relate to others meaningfully are but a few of His many gifts to us. God's love and care extend to all! Christ commanded His followers, "Love your enemies! Pray for those who persecute you! In that way you will be acting as true sons of your Father in heaven. For he gives his sunlight to both the evil and the good, and sends rain on the just and on the unjust too."[8] Those who open themselves to His love find life; those who close themselves determine their own eventual destruction. But God's love and care are always there, providing the sunshine and the rain — the essentials of life on this planet for all.

Coupled with the limits of our own humanity is the reality that we live in a "fallen" world. God has not abandoned His world, nor has He withdrawn His goodness from it. Moral evil and natural evil are present, however, and every man has and will be deeply affected by both.[9] We cannot escape our environment any more than we can escape our own nature. All will be touched by difficulties and tragedies — our own or those of ones we love.

No one will be exempt from difficult circumstances, but we need not be defeated by them.

Questions for Personal Reflection
and Group Interaction

1. Are you aware of ever having felt that somehow you would be the exception and miss all of life's tragedies?
2. Has it ever looked as if all of life's tragedies were coming to you? Did you get angry about it, or frightened, or depressed? What helped you recover from such distress?
3. Have you ever felt that you were the only person in the world to whom a particular tragedy or disappointment ever happened?
4. What positive things has suffering brought into your life?

19. When It Rains, It Pours!

AT TIMES THERE SEEMS to be no end to the occurrence of crises in our lives. While I was writing this book, we lost Verdell's father; one uncle had a serious heart attack and is not expected to live; another uncle was knocked off his tractor by a tree limb, his leg severed by the shredder; and the seven-year-old daughter of a Christian Concern director was killed in an accident, while another director's nine-year-old daughter had a stroke, paralyzing her entire right side. Sometimes life moves along rather smoothly, devoid of critical moments or calamity. Then — WHAM! — here comes a relentless series of crises.

One crisis does not wait until another is resolved to occur. Each one brings its own cargo of stress, and the stress can build up and become too much for us. Unless we learn how to work through the overload properly, we may end up physically ill or emotionally depressed.

Dr. Thomas Holmes, professor of psychiatry at the University of Washington School of Medicine in Seattle, has worked out a system which suggests the amount of stress certain crises create.[1]

Rank	Crisis	Points
1	Death of a spouse	100
2	Divorce	73
3	Marital separation	65
4	Jail term	63
5	Death of close family member	63
6	Personal injury or illness	53
7	Marriage	50
8	Job firing	47
9	Marital reconciliation	45
10	Retirement	45
11	Change in health of family member	44
12	Pregnancy	44
13	Sexual difficulties	39
14	Gain of new family member	39
15	Business readjustment	39
16	Change in financial state	38
17	Death of close friend	37
18	Change to different line of work	36
19	Change in number of arguments with spouse	35
20	Mortgage more than $10,000	31
21	Foreclosure of mortgage or loan	30
22	Change in responsibilities at work	29
23	Departure of son or daughter from home	29
24	Trouble with in-laws	29
25	Outstanding personal achievement	28
26	Wife's beginning or stopping work	26
27	Beginning or end of school	26
28	Change in living conditions	25
29	Change of personal habits	24
30	Trouble with boss	23
31	Change in work hours or conditions	20
32	Change in residence	20
33	Change in schools	20
34	Change in recreation	19
35	Change in church activities	19
36	Change in social activities	18
37	Mortgage or loan less than $10,000	17
38	Change in sleeping habits	16
39	Change in number of family gatherings	15
40	Change in eating habits	15

41	Vacation	13
42	Christmas	12
43	Minor violations of the law	11

Different individuals would rank each crisis differently, because the impact of the change would differ according to our experience, values, and responses. Nevertheless, this scale illustrates that crises do produce different amounts of stress. Dr. Holmes established an Illness Predictor Scale, showing that there is a high risk potential of developing major illnesses within a two-year period after accumulating a certain number of stress points.[2]

ILLNESS PREDICTOR SCALE

		Total points
	LOW	150
		175
		200
		225
	MEDIUM	250
		275
		300
		325
	HIGH	350
		375

There can be no doubt that each crisis produces stress, but our mental attitude toward these circumstances is more determinative of their final impact upon us than the circumstances themselves.

The significance of one's mental attitude can be seen in studying the following chart, which shows the characteristics of three kinds of depression.[3]

CHARACTERISTICS OF THE THREE KINDS OF DEPRESSION

	Discouragement (Mild)	Despondency (Serious)	Despair (Severe)
Mental	Self-doubt Resentment Self-pity	Self-criticism Anger Self-pity	Self-rejection Bitterness Self-pity
Physical	Loss of appetite Sleeplessness Unkempt appearance	Apathy Hypochondria "Weeps"	Withdrawal Passivity Catatonia
Emotional	Discontent Sadness Irritability	Distress Sorrow Loneliness	Hopelessness Schizophrenia Abandonment
Spiritual	Questions God's Will Displeased with God's Will Ungrateful Unbelieving	Anger at God's Will Rejects God's Will Gripes about God's Will	Resentment to Word Indifferent toward Word Unbelief in the Word

We need to be sensitive to those who are struggling and be willing to help them bear the overload of their circumstances.

When we find ourselves under that load which is too much for us, instead of allowing ourselves to be crushed, we need to open up to the resources of Christ and His people. Christ's words to His disciples are a promise to us: "I will not abandon you or leave you as orphans in the storm — I will come to you."[4] Look for Him and wait for Him. He is with you even if you do not believe it; He will help you come through the storm, provided you want to come through it.

Questions for Personal Reflection and Group Interaction

1. Have you ever experienced a time in your life when it looked as if tragedies would never cease?
2. Have you ever felt as if you might be overwhelmed by life's overload?
3. Have you been through any kind of stress recently which could be affecting you more than you are consciously aware?
4. Do you ever struggle with depression? What attitudes or actions have you found that help you move out of your depression?
5. Do you have someone to share your struggles with? How did you find such a person?
6. Is there someone who shares his struggles with you? What did you do that opened the way for him to share with you?
7. What do you need most from your sharing group tonight?

20. The Gospel of Success vs. the Gospel of Redemption

THERE IS A SUBTLE assumption that enters into our minds unawares. It is the assumption that if we are in God's will, everything we do will succeed. This is true only if we define success in God's terms — the fulfillment of His purpose in our lives. But by the world's definition of success — everything working out as we planned — the assumption is not true.

The ministry of Christ clearly demonstrates this truth. He was never outside the will of His Father, yet He tasted the bitterness of failure. Theologians call it "the collapse of the Great Galilean Ministry." The experience is found in the sixth chapter of John's Gospel.

For eighteen months or more, Christ had been carrying on His ministry in Galilee with visible results. Large numbers of people were coming to hear Him. A great multitude of people followed Him because they saw the miracles He performed for the diseased. The Lord, concerned for all of man's needs, fed the multitude with a boy's lunch of five barley loaves and two small fish. The people were so impressed that they wanted to make Him king. Men have always responded to the promise of something for nothing; whoever feeds us bread for which we have not labored gets our vote.

Christ refused to be a "bread messiah." He left the crowd and went up into the mountain alone. That evening the disciples crossed the sea toward Capernaum, and Christ walked to them on the water. After He reassured them that it really was He, they gladly received Him into the boat. The next day the people crossed the sea seeking Jesus. When they found Him, Christ confronted them with their inadequate motives: "The truth of the matter is that you want to be with me because I fed you, not because you believe in me."[1]

Jesus declared Himself to be the Bread which came down from heaven to nourish their souls, not just their bodies. After a discussion concerning His mission, He told them clearly they must "eat His flesh and drink His blood" to have life — that is, they must open themselves in faith to Him to such an extent that His purposes, goals, and values become theirs. The people murmured, "This is a hard saying; who can listen to it?"[2] His demand was too much for them: "After this many of his disciples drew back and no longer went about with him."[3] The multitudes also faded, and from this moment on, Christ was a fugitive, with the Pharisees and other religious leaders building up their case against Him.

The pain of rejection was real. From a human viewpoint He had failed. He was left with the Twelve, and He turned to them and asked, "Will you also go away?" It is a great letdown to see the multitude dwindle until none are left except the handful of men you started with.

Peter's affirmation was good news indeed to Christ at that moment. "Lord, to whom shall we go? You have the words of eternal life; and we have believed, and have come to know, that you are the Holy One of God."[4]

The Lord warned about the problem of success in Luke 10. He chose seventy disciples and sent them out in pairs to all the towns and villages He would later visit. When they returned, they were rejoicing in their successes. Christ said to them, "Nevertheless do not rejoice in this, that the spirits are subject to you; but rejoice that your names are written in heaven."[5]

Success at any price is a real temptation. Once God blesses

us with success, the temptation may be to focus our attention on the success rather than on Christ and our continued obedience to Him. *What if He chooses to take us through a series of failures in order to discipline and equip us with sensitivity and humility for the tasks ahead?* He has done it before and no doubt will again. Consider the life of Abraham Lincoln:

> [His] political career seemed to be one long, dreary series of failures, and he could have parked by any one of them.
>
> His first effort in political life ended in defeat. He ran for the state legislature in Illinois and was defeated — chalk up failure number one. He tried his hand at business and failed — failure number two. He was elected to Congress in 1846 but was defeated for re-election — failure number three. He tried then to get an appointment with the United States land office — failure. In 1856 he was beaten as a candidate for the Vice-presidency, and two years later he went down to defeat again before Stephen Douglas.
>
> It looks as if the man would have known when he was whipped. After so many defeats and failures, how could he ever try again? Why didn't he just park?
>
> But no. Came 1860 and the nomination as candidate for the Presidency of the United States. Would he fail again? Would he go down in defeat once more?
>
> You know what happened. And the thousands from all over the world who every year look at that brooding genius as he sits in stone in the Lincoln Memorial in Washington, D.C., know that his ultimate success after so many failures was not only a personal victory, and not merely a victory for a torn and strife-ridden nation, but a victory for all mankind.[6]

God alone is qualified to judge the real success or failure in our journey. Obedience to Him is the essence of true success. Attention from men must always remain secondary. A good soldier carries out orders regardless of whether those orders are giving him personal success.

The good news of Christ is redemptive in nature, and His redemptive purpose for us may run contrary to the American gospel of success. The question is, Are we willing to go with Him against our culture and even the opinion of our friends if necessary? That is a hard question which only the grace of God enables us to answer in the affirmative.

Questions for Personal Reflection and Group Interaction

1. How would you define success?
2. On a scale from 0 to 10, which number best represents your sense of success?
3. Have you ever experienced a failure that turned out to be a success or prepared you for a successful endeavor?
4. What do you do with your failures? Do you learn from them, or do you allow them to diminish your confidence?
5. Have you ever experienced the pain of rejection? How did you handle it? Has it left any unresolved problems for you?

21. How Do You Handle Your Crises?

WE REALLY COPE WITH our crises the way we cope with life. The intensity of our effort is the factor that changes when our situation becomes critical.

Job is an excellent example. He was a man of faith, and he enjoyed the good things of life that God bestowed upon him. Then disaster struck. He lost his possessions; overnight he fell from wealth to poverty. That was not all. He lost his seven sons and three daughters in a storm. Job's response to this dreadful news was to rend his mantle — the acknowledged sign of mourning and of the disorganization of life — and to shave his head to express his deep sense of loss.

There was no explanation for the tragedy. How would he handle it? Being a man of faith, Job fell to the ground and worshiped God saying, "Naked came I out of my mother's womb, and naked shall I return thither: the LORD gave, and the LORD hath taken away; blessed be the name of the LORD."[1] Job acknowledged God's right to order the events of his life. Job was responding to his crises the same way he had been responding to life — trusting himself and his destiny in the hands of God. ☆ Amen!

That was not the end of it. Satan challenged God again with regard to Job. "Skin for skin, yea, all that a man hath will he give for his life. But put forth thine hand now, and touch his bone and his flesh, and he will curse thee to thy face."[2] God had more faith than that in Job, and He allowed Satan to inflict him with boils from his head to his feet. Pain and misery were his to endure. His wife even prodded him, "Do you still hold fast your integrity? Curse God, and die."[3]

Job may have felt like doing just that at times, but he had lived by his trust in the character of God and, if need be, he would die by it. His response to his wife was clear: "You speak as a foolish woman. What do you expect? Shall we receive only good at the hand of God, and shall we not receive evil?"[4] God can use in a positive fashion even the evil which comes, just as the refiner purifies gold by intense heat. But we must remain *open* to Him and to life for the good to emerge.

God's servant accepted his plight as part of the life process. Job had matured sufficiently to make allowances for the rough places. His faith could bend without breaking!

Job struggled to find the reason for his suffering. But the unreasonableness of his situation in his own mind could not drive him from God. Job asked, "Why?" *The Lord did not answer the why, but did something much greater – He revealed Himself to Job.* History is filled with men who met God out of great suffering. In finding God, they were at peace with themselves and with their situation and were able to give to the world the fruit of their suffering — gifts that would not have been theirs to give had they not struggled intensely. Job's affirming statement to the Lord was, "I have heard of thee by the hearing of the ear: but now mine eye seeth thee."[5]

To see God — to know that He is and that He cares about you — transcends every question, every doubt, and every struggle!

If this seems unbelievable to you, it is because the god in your thoughts is too small to be the God of the Universe. All who have perceived Him and His character have been deeply moved. Remember when Moses asked to see God? The Lord put him in the cleft of the rock and allowed him to see His moral character, but not His whole self. No man can see God in all His fullness without being totally overwhelmed. At the end of the experience, the Scriptures say that "Moses made haste, and bowed his head toward the earth, and worshipped."[6]

If you find God in your struggle, the struggle, as real as it is, will be secondary. Your life will take on a quality that is indestructible. Your life will have meaning that transcends your suffering and will richly bless those you touch.

We add a postscript here. God permits us to ask *why*. He is not insensitive to our struggling or our suffering. He knows that from deep inside comes a need to search for a reason. Sometimes we may find a reason that satisfies our minds; we may discover we have made some wrong decisions, or that someone else has and we are being affected by them.

There will be times, however, when we cannot discern a reason for our dilemma. At these times we may question the fairness of the situation and may even doubt God's love. It does not disturb God for us to question Him. He knows that His love for us is real, and He experiences our agony more fully than we do. It is as we remain open and honest with Him about our feelings and our needs that He will, in His own way and time, make His care for us known.

Unfortunately faith — living one's life in complete trust in God's love and care — is not the only life-style we witness in the world. Let us examine some typical ways we may be tempted to choose for handling our crises.

1. *The escapist style* is characteristic of one who runs away from reality and responsibility if it brings possible pain. The escapist may leave town to get away from debt or to avoid a confrontation with his boss. Or, he may bodily stay where he is but refuse to allow any unpleasantness to penetrate him. He builds walls around himself and refuses to deal with the problem at hand. His wife or parents or a friend may have to work on solving the problem, but they need not expect any help from the escapist until he is willing to stop running and deal with life as it is. The tragedy is that the person who constantly runs from life never really lives.

2. *The fighter pits himself against everyone and everything that gets in his way.* He seeks power and domination over his environment, for power brings control. If he can control, he can manipulate the events of his life so that he is always on top, regardless of how many others he may put on the bottom. Unhealthy competition and conflict distinguish his style. The fighter can never admit weakness or failure. If things do not work out, it's always someone else's fault. He is dead serious, and his objective is to win at any price. The tragedy here is that he never really knows himself or others. There will be much action and interaction, but little depth.

3. *Becoming the victim* is the third pattern. The victim handles life by absorbing insults — accepting woes and hurts without responding. He cops out. "What does it matter anyway? Whatever I could do wouldn't change a thing." That's the way he feels, and he drags along complaining and whimpering about the hard knocks of life. The tragedy is that the victim never discovers the potency of his life.

4. *The happy-go-lucky style* may look good to many of us, but it also lacks reality. This is the person who refuses to acknowledge the presence of pain. He does not deal with the whole of life, but only with that part with which he feels comfortable. When a severe crisis comes his way, he will become an escapist if at all possible. The tragedy in this instance is that he never develops the kind of sensitivity that enables him to understand, identify, or communicate with others, or even with himself.

It is obvious that none of the styles we have listed are adequate descriptions of any of us. We are too complicated to be described in such simplistic terms. But we may recognize ourselves in them and become aware of the ways in which we are tempted to cope with life's hard places unrealistically. If so, dare to face your conflict as it is and plant your life firmly in the care and character of God.

Questions for Personal Reflection and Group Interaction

1. How do you respond to your crises?
2. How did your parents handle their crises?

3. Can you identify with any of the various approaches often taken in dealing with crises mentioned in this chapter?
4. Have you ever had an experience that caused you to question God's love for you? Were you able to work through your struggle sufficiently to accept your plight as a part of life and not as the absence of God's care for you?
5. What have you found to be most helpful in coping with tough circumstances?

22. Coping With Senseless Tragedy

IN OUR LIVES, EVENTS occur that many would call "senseless tragedy." Jack and Nancé Wilson, two of the founders of Christian Concern Foundation and close friends of our family, recently experienced an unspeakable tragedy: their seven-year-old daughter was killed in a motorcycle accident. The loss was great. The hurt was deep. What possible purpose could such an event have? Life held so much promise for Brenda. She was an exceptionally bright child with a warm, outgoing personality, a delight to all who knew her. Why should her life be cut short — only seven years! Where could an answer be found? Was it a *senseless* tragedy? More important, where were the resources for enduring such grief?

I think it is helpful to share some of the feelings and experiences that Nancé has expressed. In her poems you will see something of the spirit of this little girl and the deep faith of her parents.

> She had had a spanking
> And it made her mad —

165

at herself
at me.
She slammed her door
    and cried
And stayed in her room
    awhile
Working it out.

"I wanted to write a mad letter,"
    she said,
"But Jesus said, 'That wouldn't
    be friendly.'"
So she wrote a friendly one
    It said
    I LOVE JACK AND NANCÉ
    THEY LOVE ME, TOO —
    JESUS LOVES JACK, NANCÉ
AND BRENDA — AND
TINY TIM, TOO.

                * * *

We were shopping and we bought a balloon
    With a painted "LOVE,"
    A rabbit inside
    With helium
    And a string —

To her it was a lively thing —
A playmate — fun and free.
"Come on Daddy," she said,
    Eager
    Alive
    Joyful and
    Certain,
"Let's let it go" — they did,
    and watched it disappear.
Symbolic of what I had to do – with her.

Yes, they had to watch her disappear — without any explanation
from life or God or anyone else. Although they could not answer
adequately the why of this tragedy, their faith is allowing meaning to
emerge from her life and her death that is redemptive. Neither her
life nor her death was wasted! In her living she brought great joy, and
in her dying she brought a fresh dependency upon God. A rich legacy
indeed!

The event may be an illness or an accident, a death or a "Dear John" letter, the loss of a job or a policeman at the door, but it comes with the force of a hurricane and threatens to break us apart. At that moment we may be able to identify with the painful experiences of the psalmist: "I am exhausted and crushed; I groan in despair. Lord, you know how I long for my health once more. You hear my every sigh. My heart beats wildly, my strength fails, and I am going blind. My loved ones and friends stay away, fearing my disease. Even my own family stands at a distance."[1] There may come a sense of desperate aloneness and helplessness as we face happenings we cannot control.

We cannot always choose our circumstances but we can choose our attitudes toward those circumstances. Viktor Frankl, writing about the horrors he and others experienced in a German concentration camp, stated,

> We who lived in concentration camps can remember the men who walked through the huts comforting others, giving away their last piece of bread. They may have been few in number, but they offer sufficient proof that everything can be taken from a man but one thing: the last of the human freedoms — to choose one's attitude in any given set of circumstances, to choose one's own way. . . . Even though conditions such as lack of sleep, insufficient food and various mental stresses may suggest that the inmates were bound to react in certain ways, in the final analysis it becomes clear that the sort of person the prisoner became was the result of an inner decision, and not the result of camp influences alone. Fundamentally, therefore, any man can, even under such circumstances, decide what shall become of him — mentally and spiritually.[2]

What are some common attitudes that emerge under severe pressure?

1. We may decide that life is hard and cruel and become angry at God for allowing such a thing to occur.

2. We may close ourselves to life and allow our difficult circumstances to make us bitter and resentful toward all, especially those who are enjoying life.

3. We may turn our anger or hurt inward and blame ourselves for the mishap and spend the rest of our years punishing ourselves for it.

4. We may decide that life has no meaning and no God

and wander in unbelief.

5. We may move ahead in faith and experience the life-giving resources of God. Let me emphasize that the greatest resource God offers to us is Himself. He comes to us Himself to comfort, heal, encourage, and restore us — not just to the place we were, but to a place of greater wholeness, sensitivity, and hope. God chose to suffer in order to relieve our suffering and give meaning to it. In the cross of Christ we see the extent to which God gives Himself to us — the depth of His love and involvement in our predicament. He is reaching out for you, now! Will you reach out to Him and ask Him to help you find His way through your difficulty?

Let me define *faith* for you in the context of a crisis.

1. Crisis is a signal to the person of faith to stop where he is and listen. We may have become so preoccupied with the things of life and with our plans and projects that we have lost our focus and may not know where we are personally or what our resources are. Faith will enable us to do as the psalmist suggests: "Stand silent! Know that I am God!" In knowing that God *is* and that He knows the darkness through which we are passing, we can take courage and affirm our dependency and trust in Him. Listen to the psalmist's experience and affirmation of faith:

> God is our refuge and strength, a tested help in times of trouble. And so we need not fear even if the world blows up, and the mountains crumble into the sea. Let the oceans roar and foam; let the mountains tremble!
>
> There is a river of joy flowing through the City of our God — the sacred home of the God above all gods. God himself is living in that City; therefore it stands unmoved despite the turmoil everywhere. He will not delay his help. The nations rant and rave in anger — but when God speaks, the earth melts in submission and kingdoms totter into ruin.
>
> The Commander of the armies of heaven is here among us. He, the God of Jacob, has come to rescue us. Come, see the glorious things that our God does, how he brings ruin upon the world, and causes wars to end throughout the earth, breaking and burning every weapon. "Stand silent! Know that I am God! I will be honored by every nation in the world!"
>
> The Commander of the heavenly armies is here among us! He, the God of Jacob, has come to rescue us![3]

When our world falls apart, we desperately need something or someone who can give us a sense of stability, an awareness that here is one who can hold us up and who will not leave us alone. Faith's object of trust is Jesus Christ, and He can be counted on even if the world blows up! Without Him and the people through whom He ministers to us, we would have only despair. But He comes to give us hope and the resources for a new beginning.

2. In crises, faith looks for God's alternatives to futility and despair. He always has one. We may not see it immediately, but as we look to Him, a creative alternative will come in time regardless of how hopeless our situation may look. We may be facing death — our own — and discover that God's alternative is life — life beyond the grave in His presence where there are no more tears, or pain or death, but joy unspeakable and life filled with potential beyond our wildest dreams. That promise and that hope take the sting out of death.

We may be facing a situation that seems so hard that we feel unable to move beyond it. We may fear that there does not exist a meaningful life for us beyond our tragedy. Yet some fulfillment always comes for those who remain open to life and to God. It will take time for the wounds to heal and one's spirit to revive, but they will heal, provided you do not cling to your crushing experience and refuse to get well.

3. Faith enables us to see that nothing in our experience is wasted. It is not the hardship but the feeling that nothing ultimately matters that defeats us. As we have indicated, faith does not necessarily furnish us the reasons for our calamity, but it does provide the resources for surviving them. It is faith that enables us to declare, "We know that in everything God works for good with those who love him, who are called according to his purpose."[4]

Not everything is good. Not everything that happens to us is good. No, we live in a fallen world; evil is a part of the present reality. We are selfish people living among selfish people. But in everything we open to God He does something redemptive in it, and in us, and brings good from it.

The redemptive possibilities are limitless. Being caught by the power of alcohol is tragic, but friends who by God's grace through Alcoholics Anonymous have recovered have found a ministry to other alcoholics that no nonalcoholic can duplicate. They understand the problem because they have been there. God is bringing good out of their problem.

I have seen a mother who lost her child bring comfort to another who lost hers in a way that neither I nor anyone else could, who had not been through such distress. *Wounds healed form scars of strength.*

It is true that we prefer to do without the wound or even the strength it can potentially bring, but as human beings we do not have that alternative. Pain comes to all. Our only option is whether we allow pain to immobilize and destroy us, or whether we find a way to survive and make creative use of it. That choice really is ours.

4. By faith we understand that this life does not contain the whole story. We are as Abraham, "waiting expectantly and confidently, looking forward to the city which has fixed and firm foundations, whose Architect and Builder is God."[5] There is the promise of eternal life, in which all inequities will be resolved and life itself will be inexhaustibly rich and full. Without this dimension, the problem of suffering and evil is without a complete answer. With it, we have the assurance that one day we will understand, and the wrong will be made right.

Questions for Personal Reflection and Group Interaction

1. Have you ever experienced a tragedy that seemed senseless? What were your feelings — hurt? anger? bitterness?
2. Did you ever experience a sense of peace and hope as you attempted to work through your loss? From what source did this peace and hope come?
3. Has the wound healed? How do you know it has, or how do you know it has not?
4. Who was most helpful to you in the accepting, healing process? What did they do?
5. What did you learn about yourself? about God? about your need for the support of others?
6. Have you been better able to help someone else as a result of your loss experience?

7. Can you identify with any of the common attitudes that emerge under severe pressure, such as those mentioned in this chapter?
8. What resources for coping with tough circumstances has your faith brought to you?
9. Have you come to terms with the reality that pain is part of life and that our only option is whether we allow it to immobilize and destroy us, or we find a way to survive and make creative use of it?
10. Whether or not you have faced a tragedy, how would you go about being supportive and helping someone else through a tragedy?
11. Do you believe there is life beyond the grave in which all inequities will be resolved and life, for God's people, will be inexhaustibly rich and full?

23. The Loss of Meaning

THE LOSS OF MEANING is perhaps the most devastating crisis of all. Viktor Frankl's experience as a prisoner in a Nazi concentration camp bears witness to this fact. He writes that life in those camps tore open the human soul and exposed its depths. Many died. Those who survived, survived on hope alone. When a man could no longer make sense out of his suffering in those camps, he was finished.

> Any attempt to restore a man's inner strength in the camp had first to succeed in showing him some future goal. . . . "He who has a *why* to live for can bear with almost any how." . . . Whenever there was an opportunity for it, one had to give them a *why* — an aim — for their lives, in order to strengthen them to bear the terrible *how* of their existence. Woe to him who saw no more sense in his life, no aim, no purpose, and therefore no point in carrying on. He was soon lost.[1]

One of the most distraught persons I have seen in my counseling said, "I have no future. Life holds nothing for me. I have achieved all my goals and they are empty. And even worse, there is nothing I want to do, nowhere I want to go. *Everything is meaning-*

less!" Such despair often leads to suicide, and in this country between 50,000 and 70,000 persons commit suicide every year. A much larger number make an attempt without succeeding. They do not have a *why* for living that enables them to choose life over death, even if life seems unbearable at that moment.

The loss of meaning can be much less dramatic than the experience in the concentration camp or the counseling situation I just related. It may appear in the form of Sunday afternoon blahs. We can fill our lives so full of frenzied activities that we lose contact with ourselves and become impoverished human beings. When all the activity halts and we have an afternoon to ourselves — with nothing to do, no one to impress or to please — the emptiness becomes painfully apparent.

One indication of this inner vacuum is boredom. One psychiatrist has noted that boredom is now causing, and certainly bringing to psychiatrists, more problems to solve than does distress. It is tragic when one's life does not have enough content to make it at least interesting, if not exciting.

There are some external reasons for the loss of meaning in our day.

1. The concept of determinism so prevalent today shuts man up to nothingness. To think of man as only the product of his heredity and environment without the freedom to be different erases meaning from his existence and fosters a sense of fatalism. Our culture has an overdose of this pessimistic view of man, and it has been strengthened by a psychotherapy that sees man as simply a complex composite of conditioned reflexes. Frankl writes,

> To be sure, a human being is a finite being, and his freedom is restricted. It is not freedom from conditions, but freedom to take a stand toward the conditions. . . . As a professor in two fields, neurology and psychiatry, I am fully aware of the extent to which man is subject to biological, psychological and sociological conditions. But in addition to being a professor in two fields I am a survivor of four camps — concentration camps that is — and as such I also bear witness to the unexpected extent to which man is capable of defying and braving even the worst conditions conceivable.[2]

From the biblical viewpoint, man has a will that he can exercise freely, and he is responsible whether he gives in to the forces which influence and press against him or rises above them. Moses is but one example of a man who refused an opportunity that by the world's standards was unequaled in his day. "It was by faith that Moses, when he grew up, refused to be treated as the grandson of the king, but chose to share ill-treatment with God's people instead of enjoying the fleeting pleasures of sin."[3] Man does have a part in his own destiny. He has the freedom to choose his way, and all of heaven or hell will support him in it.

2. Technology has contributed to man's loss of meaning. The computer can store and retrieve more information in seconds than a man can in a lifetime. Automation of every kind eliminates the need for more and more man-hours. The result is that the man who has not found a solid spiritual foundation for his life is being intimidated by the machine. Without spiritual dimension, man's value is limited to his ability to perform.

3. The destruction of our traditions and our heroes has contributed enormously to the lack of meaning prevalent in our day. In discovering that our heroes were, after all, human, we moved from adoration to contempt for them. Seeing people who in spite of their problems made great contributions to mankind should have encouraged us who are aware of the limitations of our own humanity to attempt the same. Instead we became cynical and distrustful.

Rather than trying to reform our traditions, we have attempted to destroy them completely. One radical student said to me, "We ought to burn all our traditions and start over." I asked him what he thought we should start over with, and he said, "I don't know; I haven't thought about that." *Man cannot exist in a vacuum, yet we have created an emotional void.* What remains that evokes undying loyalty? Who do you admire enough to emulate? What positive life-building projects are you engaged in?

Remember that life becomes self-destructive when it is lived for self alone.

Let us consider some common internal contributors to the loss of meaning.

1. It is common to have achieved one's goals and find these goals inadequate. Many men who develop only their aggressive

and masculine side, giving all their time and energy to their professions and to building economic security, end up on top with no place to go. The excitement of being on the way up is gone, and now everything is monotonous.

2. Having an unrealistic goal and, after years of struggle, giving up hope of ever reaching it may leave one with a sense of stark futility. One may realize that he will never be famous or rich or president of his company or have his own company or whatever. His purpose has been frustrated, and he feels like a failure. His confidence may fall to zero and with it his motivation. "Why go on, what's left for me?" will be his haunting question.

Let's face it: not everyone is going to end up atop the pyramid, even if it's a small pyramid. But life can have meaning even at the bottom of the ladder! It may be easier to find the real meaning in one's existence if there is not so much success as to get in the way of the search.

3. Losing a spouse or someone very close can leave a person without a sense of significance. It hurts to lose those we love. Everyone takes a substantial amount of meaning for his existence from his love relationships. Frankl points out from his prison experience that the hope that a loved one was waiting for them on the outside gave sufficient reason for their continued endurance. The Christian faith speaks beautifully to this loss in two ways: first, the realization that the love we have shared with another person is eternal and can never be lost; second, the realization that for the Christian the separation is only temporary.

Responses to this inner loss of meaning vary. Some try to compensate for the emptiness they feel by acquiring more things. Materialism is a poor substitute for authentic existence and becomes a hard taskmaster.

Others try to fill the void with pleasure: more entertainment, more thrills, more alcohol, more drugs, more sex — anything to help one forget his meaninglessness. The problem is that these diversions are only temporary, and after they pass, the feeling of nothingness will have increased. I know it is a human trait to feel that we will be the exception — that we can do certain things which may harm others but not us. Somehow we can have our fling and our fun and come out on the other side unaffected. I admit my experience is limited, but after fifteen years of counseling I have yet to meet the exception. The price paid for self-indulgence and for exploiting others is extremely high. The kickback may not come immediately, giving us a false sense of well-being, but it will come.

Perhaps the greatest tragedy of all is to have destroyed enough of the self, made in God's image, that we cannot even recognize the fruit of our selfish pleasure. It is possible to become so insensitive that we look upon all others as stupid and out of step.

The values we answer to with our lives, not just our words, reveal the content of our meaning. In an early-morning group we were instructed to list our priorities. Each week for three weeks we recorded and reported to the group the way we spent our time, e.g., the amount of time spent with our spouse, our children, at work, with our clients, in personal and spiritual reflection, on recreation, rest, social activities.

The assignment was revealing. Our stated list of priorities did not coincide with reality more than half the time. We discovered that unconsciously we were allowing circumstances to dictate priorities — whatever or whoever was making the loudest noise and exerting the greatest pressure received our time and attention. We found that we were not living intentionally.

None of us need be reminded of what can happen to marriages or to children when priorities are determined by circumstances. The pressure of a person's vocation can lead him down the blind alley of neglect unless he takes deliberate steps to prevent it.

Make a list of your priorities and for one week record how you spend your time. See if you need to make some changes!

Man is unique among all the creatures that inhabit the earth, and part of his uniqueness is the need to make sense out of his existence. He alone can ask of any event, "What does this mean?" He can then integrate his past, present, and future around his answer. Practically speaking, every man has *answered* to some degree the question of meaning, i.e., he has a view of life and the universe that reflect his effort to relate to the totality of his experience. Even if he says life is meaningless, he has judged his own existence and is left with a world view of absurdity.

Man also has the freedom and the responsibility to choose his viewpoint; it is not thrust upon him as something inevitable. We need to be reminded that we do not go out one day and choose our philosophy of life as we do a book. We acquire it in bits and pieces from our parents, teachers, and peers, from our experiences, dreams, and hopes. We may have been hurt or disappointed and gained a negative viewpoint, or we may have been encouraged and loved and gained a positive one. We could have been influenced by a teacher who planted in our minds a dream that became the basis for interpreting life. We may never recognize all the sources of our particular perspective of life, but we can and must evaluate that perspective as we mature.

Christians have a great advantage in their potential for finding a creative view of life and history. We have in our possession the Bible, which is both the record of God's self-revelation and part of that revelation and as such purposes to bring us into a right relationship with God. Such a relationship does not eliminate but heightens the mystery and the drama of life. In our pilgrimage of faith we can begin to understand from the Bible the unfolding of God's redemptive purpose; we discover that we, ourselves, have been caught up in that drama.[4]

History has a destination, and so do we. All of life is pregnant with meaning. Not one single event is senseless, though we may be unable within our limitations to understand or explain every event. God is up to something big through Christ in your life, in history, and in eternity! Christ's description of His mission is that of giving to us *abundant life* — life that is full, real, great!

Think of it: the God who planned the intricate details of the universe has a unique purpose for you. You can understand that His dream for you is to share in His very life as His child; in the ages to come you, along with the rest of His people, will be the medium through which He will express His endless creativity and His inexhaustible love.

Along with God's call to become a believer come specific tasks to perform. I cannot tell you what yours are, and you cannot define mine. As we walk by faith, digging into the Scriptures and seeking to be open to Him and to the opportunities that unfold, we can begin to recognize specific tasks as God's assignment for us. This assignment may entail great adventure in the eyes of the world, or it may involve great suffering. But the realization that we have a place in God's history makes it meaningful beyond description.

Questions for Personal Reflection and Group Interaction

1. Do you have a "why" to live that will enable you to bear almost any "how"? What is it?
2. Have you ever experienced arriving at your goal, only to discover that it was not what you expected?
3. Is boredom a problem for you?
4. Do you feel that you have the power to effect significant changes in your own future and destiny? Or do you feel that you are being carried along by forces over which you have no control?
5. Have you ever felt that your worth could be measured only in terms of your productivity, i.e., what you could produce?
6. When you discover that a person has a weakness in some aspect of his life, do you lose all confidence in him?
7. Have you ever lost someone or something which caused you to feel that your life would never again have significance?
8. Do you allow your circumstances to dictate your priorities?
9. Has your imagination ever been captivated by a great purpose? What?
10. Do you suppose that if the Christian message is true, God must have a magnificent purpose in mind for you?

24. Recovering From a Moral Failure

"CAN YOU TELL ME HOW I can maintain a meaningful relationship with my wife and continue my affair with my secretary?" the distinguished man in his mid-thirties asked me. He and his wife had come to me for counsel two years earlier. Their marriage was on the verge of collapse, and they came as the last resort before calling it quits. After dealing with some of their hostility, they decided to try to make their marriage work.

As happens so often, the couple failed to fulfill their commitments to each other, and the old pattern of going separate ways soon returned. The husband's promiscuous sexual habits also continued. Now he was back in my office, facing again the crisis of a moral collapse that left him uncommitted on all fronts and very miserable. He indicated that nothing seemed to hold meaning for him — neither his relationships nor his profession. Yet he wanted to hold onto his wife, because she loved him and he knew it; *and* his mistress, who offered him alluring diversion from the emptiness he felt.

He asked for my opinion, and I shared with him that there was no way to my knowledge that he could make such an arrangement work. God made us for maximum living; to violate His revelation of what makes life work best is to violate both ourselves and His moral law. *Morals do not make life harder, but happier and healthier.* Of course, telling another person what is right as you understand right does not change him. Each has freedom to act as he chooses, but we do not have the power to control the consequences of those actions. What we sow we reap; when we sow wildly to the wind we reap the whirlwind.[1]

Somehow this man believed he could make it work and refused help. You can guess the outcome. He lost his wife and children first, then his mistress. He has wounds that will probably take years to heal, if they ever do. The price for becoming a law unto ourselves is high indeed.

We do have a very positive standard of right and wrong in the Bible. Some have twisted it into a legalism that has turned many others from it. But to look at the ethics of the Christian faith as revealed in the Scriptures is to see the wisdom of God being exercised for man's good.[2]

Others whom I have counseled defended their immoral activity on the grounds of having lost all affection for their spouse. In the fury of one's uninhibited passions it is difficult to distinguish love from lust and even more difficult to know *who*, if anyone, is loved. I have observed numerous cases wherein, once the affair cooled, the offending spouse discovered he did love his wife. But while the affair was going strong, he swore he had no feelings for his mate.

I always suggest that a person who really wants to know if he has any affection left for his wife break off the affair at least long enough for it to cool; then he should ask himself whom he really wants to share his life with. Such a question is pointless as long as the affair is alive.

I am reminded of a man who divorced his wife and married his mistress. After a relatively short time he confided that had he tried half as hard in his first marriage as he was trying in his second, he would have had a super relationship with his first wife.

The old saying, The grass looks greener on the other side of the fence, has great validity. Many have discovered to their dismay just how deceiving looks can be.

Dishonesty in business seems to be a great weakness today. The pressures come from every side and will eventually engulf us unless we make some prior commitments that are positive and definitive and we stay with them. Any evasion that violates the truth is always a step downward. Although we may cringe at that first step, each succeeding one will be easier. Few people, including hardened criminals, ever intended to go the extreme in the beginning. Evil has a way of working faster than good, and it keeps luring us to discard each moral limit we accept for ourselves. It will destroy us in the end if it goes unchecked.

We can be grateful that God is at work, attempting to gain our attention without violating our freedom, so that He might reverse this downward spiral and enable us to face ourselves, others, and our world honestly and openly without guile. It takes years to build a good reputation, but only minutes to destroy it.

What can we do when we find ourselves faced with a moral failure? We will all face this crisis; we will make mistakes and fail. Our failures may or may not be obvious, but there will be failures, for perfection awaits the next life. The guilt and alienation that come with our failures are a crushing load to carry. As Huck Finn said, "Sometimes a feller's conscience takes up more room than all the rest of a person's insides."

We have several options: (1) We can deny that we made a mistake; (2) we can lay the blame on someone else or on our circumstances; (3) we can attempt to make our behavior acceptable to ourselves and perhaps even to others by rationalizing; (4) we can face up to our failure, ask for forgiveness, and make retribution whenever it's possible to do so.

God offers us forgiveness and the resources for beginning again. *Praise God*

Questions for Personal Reflection
and Group Interaction

1. How do you determine "right and wrong" for yourself and others — on the basis of what you want and feel you can get by with; on the basis of what others are doing or the mores of your culture; on the ethics of your family or your religious commitment; or what?

2. Are you willing for others — such as your spouse, children, employer, employees, and friends — to operate within the same moral standard as you do? If they did, would their conduct enrich or diminish your life?

3. Do you believe there are moral absolutes? Why, or why not? Can society exist without constructive morals?

4. Have you ever studied the Judeo-Christian ethic from the perspective of helping people maintain mental, moral, and spiritual health? From the perspective of building high-trust, low-fear relationships?

5. Have you ever faced a major moral failure? What did you do to recover? What resources did you find most helpful?

6. Are you aware of how easy it would be to slip beyond the moral lines we have accepted for ourselves when it would be to our advantage or pleasure to do so?

7. Have you ever experienced forgiveness — God's forgiveness which enabled you to forgive yourself?

8. Do you recognize the temptation to deny, to rationalize, or to lay the blame for our own failures on another or on circumstances? Have you matured to the extent that you are committed to dealing more honestly with your failures?

25. Pain and Suffering

SUFFERING IS INEVITABLE. None of us can permanently evade it. Yet few, if any, are ever prepared for it when it comes. Our health is one of many things we take for granted. To have a body free of pain, functioning vigorously, enabling us to carry on our pursuits with great ease is an indescribable asset — though only a temporary asset in this world. Illness, accidents, and age can lay waste our bodies and minds ever so quickly.

If health is one of your hallmarks today, do not waste time brooding over the future and torturing yourself over the "what ifs" of life. *Celebrate* its gift and make good use of your energy and vigor. Regard every day of your life as an event to be celebrated, and invest it for the good of others and for the glory of God. Learning how to live life to its fullest will enable a person to suffer without bitterness. After all, if the Lord tarries, none of us will get out of this world alive anyway. Death need not be depressing! It is a statement of fact — a fact that reality verifies daily.

If suffering and pain have overtaken you in your journey

then there is good news for you. God has not forsaken you, and your suffering is not pointless. As Samuel declared, "The LORD will not forsake His people."[1]

You may cry out from the depth of your being, "Why? Why me? Why this? Why so soon?" You may feel you have only started to live and now it looks as though everything may be cut short. But the good news of Christ is that you can live meaningfully right up to your death, if death be your present assignment — and, yes, beyond!

Job asked why and rightly so. It hurt to lose everything — his wealth, his family, his friends, and his health. Although he never received an answer for the reason of his suffering, *he discovered that God was in his suffering with him, that it was not senseless, and that he could trust God beyond his limit of understanding.* As great as our pain may be, we can survive as human beings if we know that we are not alone and that from our suffering can come a quality of meaning which will redeem it from pointless agony.

Nothing is wasted in God's economy, and no need goes unnoticed! We can pray for healing and submit to the best medical help available. Yet, for reasons known only to God, some of our cries for physical healing are answered with a *yes* and others with a *no*. Of course, we are aware of the fact that, if He answered every prayer with a yes, we would stay in this world too long. With whole bodies and healthy minds, none would pray, "It is time for me to die."

This world is only a part of the picture. Here we struggle and experience life as a mixture of good and bad, hope and despair, love and selfishness. God's dream for us is to share in His life and His creative resources as His dear children, and this world is too small for the fulfillment of that dream. In this world God confronts us with Himself and His purpose, but gives us the freedom to buy into His dream by faith in His Son, Jesus Christ, or reject His love-offer and pursue our own selfish ends. That choice is ours now. To receive Christ as one's Savior and Lord does not bring immediate escape from suffering, but does bring adequate resources for enduring our agony.

Others may suffer more or less than we do. But we do well

to remember that suffering is all-encompassing. Suffering is like gas pumped into an empty room: it will fill the room completely whatever its size. Thus suffering fills the human soul, whether the suffering is great or small.

Suffering colors our whole life, but God has given us the power to choose what that color will be — darkness or light, bitterness or hope.

The experience of pain and suffering affords us an unusual opportunity to face ourselves in the core of our being. What are our strengths and weaknesses? What have we lived for and now may die for? What do we consider valuable and truly important? What are we like under great stress?

None of us is so strong that suffering will not threaten to overwhelm us at some point. But we can find, in God's suffering for us and with us, the resources for recovering our dignity and courage.

I do not want to minimize the problem. Suffering is hard — so hard it often seems unbearable and we cry, "I can't go on like this." It is at this point we need to remember that it is not so much the experiences life brings that crush us, as our attitude toward them. We can and do choose our response to life, to its experiences, and to our suffering. To give in to self-pity only destroys our opportunity to make use of the thing that is costing us our lifeblood.

We have no choice over what our suffering does to our body, but we decide what it does to our spirit. If we see ourselves as helpless victims who can do nothing to make our situation better, we may become locked into a self-defeating attitude and paralyze our capabilities of even believing that this attitude can be changed. But if we realize that we have chosen an attitude which hurts instead of helps, and we *want* to, we can change it at any given moment by simply deciding to do so. God has given us that freedom over our destiny and none can take it from us.

Frankl says, "When a man finds that it is his destiny to suffer, he will have to accept his suffering as his task; his single and unique task. . . . No one can relieve him of his suffering or suffer in his place. His unique opportunity lies in the way in which he bears his burden."[2]

A young wife and mother who lost her husband and children, and whose own body was crushed in a terrible car wreck on a railroad crossing, wrote,

> Pain? I know pain. You will know it, meet it, fight it, whoever you are. You must. It is a law of life that you must face pain. . . . I believe that, being physically constituted as we are, pain is inevitable for all of us. We are flesh, soft flesh, and we cannot possibly escape being cut on one or the other of the barbs of life.
>
> But this I have learned, in my fight with it: it is given to produce something better than tears and frustration. It produces love, sympathy and a brotherhood that is more spiritual than physical. There is deep purpose in pain; it opens our eyes to the methods of God with men. It brings out of the heart and mind the finest that God has put there. . . . [3]

George B. Lieberman wrote out of his experience of having both legs crushed and of living with pain from that day on,

> There are two ways to conquer pain: either we can try to escape it, or we can try to make it useful. . . . Pain is a cruel master. But can it not be a teacher?
>
> Yes, the first lesson it teaches is faith, religious faith. Of course, there are moments of rebellion when it seems easier to reject, to denounce — and to shake the fist against Heaven. But in the midst of despair and helplessness, the feeling that we can still lift our voices to a Power beyond ourselves, that we can still communicate our torment and our triumph to the Unseen Friend and retain a light however dim — that is faith. . . .
>
> So upon its wings of destruction, pain carries a promise. And this is the great lesson it has taught me: the promise beyond pain is life. [4]

"The promise beyond pain is life!" Pain may still be with us, but it can no longer blot out meaning or hope. It becomes redemptive, and our greatest and final gift to those we love may be the way we bear our suffering and reveal our faith.

Questions for Personal Reflection
and Group Interaction

1. Have you ever given God thanks for the health of your body?
2. Have you ever experienced anything that could have made you bitter?

3. Have you personally known someone who has lived with much suffering? What was their attitude toward their suffering? Toward others? What was your reaction to them?
4. How do you react to being ill? What kind of a patient are you?
5. Do you indulge in self-pity when you are ill?
6. Do you view yourself as a helpless victim of your illness?
7. Can you accept your suffering as a task that offers a unique opportunity to experience yourself and life at a deeper level?
8. What lessons have you learned from your suffering?

26. We Are All Growing Older

OUR CULTURE WORSHIPS youth. There are societies in our world that give the seat of highest honor to the oldest members of their clan, but not ours. We have a "throwaway" mentality that is destructive to both our natural and our human resources.

An environment such as ours contributes greatly to the fear most people have of growing older. Many of those who do not consciously fear aging simply feel that somehow it will not happen to them — illusions of immortality. But viewing the aging as we do and knowing that we will one day walk where they walk (should we live as long) can be devastating. Along with this negative attitude may be the fear of losing the physical and mental powers we now enjoy without the slightest awareness that different strengths and capacities can take their place. New gifts come with each age. Our capacities continue with some modifications. We can live, if we choose to, right up to the end of life and, yes, even through and beyond the end.

Our fear of life is the deepest root from which our fear of aging and death springs. We have not learned to trust the process, or more significantly, the God behind the process. If we would allow faith to take root in our hearts — faith that moves beyond a closed system of beliefs to that of a life-style of openness and trust in the God who is there and who loves and answers back redemptively — then the aging process could become an exciting adventure.

Preparation for aging creatively is important. When should we begin our preparation? Now. It's never too late and never too early, because the potential for wholeness in our journey resides more in the realm of attitudes than years.

In one pastorate I had a seventy-two-year-old friend who made many pastoral calls with me. He was retired from an oil company, but had more to do, according to his own comments, than ever in his life. W. E. Dickie spoke of visiting the elderly in our congregation. Many of those he included were his junior in years, but not in frame of mind. W. E. was a young, vigorous man in attitude. He took up painting at sixty-five and golf at seventy and found that he was good at both. But being good at it was not nearly so important as having the courage to risk new frontiers. His life-style included new interests and areas of exploration, and that no doubt was a major part of the secret for his physical, mental, and emotional vigor. We are never too old to be alive and interested, unless consciousness is taken away.

Another obvious secret was W. E.'s willingness to have his own ideas and perspectives stretched or even changed if the truth led in that direction. *He was flexible.* I have known few men who had stronger convictions than he, and we disagreed on a lot of matters. Yet he always wanted to explore the reasons for my conclusions, especially if they differed from his. We spent hours discussing and studying the issues. Sometimes I changed my mind, sometimes he changed his, and often neither changed. But our dialogue stimulated the flow of creative juices more than most of my classes in college or seminary. I think I learned something important from W. E. in every encounter, and he had a willingness to learn something new from a man young enough to be his grandson.

W. E. spoke often of his past, not in the sense of idealizing it or trying to relive it, but in an effort to gain perspective from it. Perspective is one of the great assets of aging. Years of experience with oneself, with others, with the living God in this world can bring much wisdom. W. E. also recognized that the most important source of wisdom is God Himself. Job said, "As you say, older men like me are wise. They understand. But true wisdom and power are God's. He alone knows what we should do; he understands."[1] James stated, "If you want to know what God wants you to do, ask him, and he will gladly tell you, for he is always ready to give a bountiful supply of wisdom to all who ask him."[2]

If we really want to know so we can act in obedience to Him to whom we have given our allegience, He will make the way clear enough for us to continue on our journey in the right direction. God may speak to us through the Scriptures, through our experiences, through another person, through our circumstances, through our desires, or through a situation in the world wherein we recognize His call to us to be His person there. He may impress us with an assignment or a direction through His Spirit within or through another channel of His choosing. Wanting to know and being open for Him to enable us to see by whatever means He chooses is the posture we need to receive His word or call. Of course, the more we learn from the Bible about God, His redemptive purpose, and His ways with men, the better equipped we will be to recognize His voice among the many other voices that clamor for our attention. Reuel Howe at sixty-eight wrote,

> The foundations of positive aging are laid in the earlier years, long before aging is a concern. A younger person, for example, who learns that the meanings of failure can be recycled into insight for growth has begun a style of life that will renew him as he moves from year to year. Instead of allowing himself to be defeated, he will wrest some triumphs and satisfactions from what may have been a bruising struggle. . . . We can choose to look for clouds or for sunshine. . . . Thus, one learns to love being old by living each day on the way with enthusiasm, by keeping in touch with one's unfolding story, and by letting tomorrow care for itself.[3]

Research indicates that aging is a gentle decline which begins around thirty. We are not young one day and old the next. There is a gradual, descending process affecting one physically that cannot be stopped. However, there can be an ascending psychological and spiritual development until the end of our days.

A rule of thumb we do well to remember is that *the human system seems to respond best to use.* Physical, mental, and spiritual exercise is important.

Another beautiful resource of the Christian faith is that for us the best is always yet to be. Hope is a fantastic gift from God! We do have a future here until He calls us home to an even greater future there. How can life break a man who is never without hope or a future?

Christ calls us to a life of love, not hate. When we exercise self-giving love, we are at our best. Each time we love, we increase our power to be — to be who God intended us to be; to be who others need us to be; to be the self that neither age nor death can diminish.

Feeling sorry for ourselves and becoming preoccupied with bodily dysfunctions and complaints is self-defeating. The body functions better, and most certainly the psyche, when we adopt the attitude that we are going to do the best we can with the powers and capacities left us until the Lord says, "It's enough," and beckons us to come to Him.

We need to invest ourselves in something that excites us. In so doing we discover that the flow of energy and vitality is greatly increased. A man I know was a pioneer in the science of developing and caring for fruit orchards. He loves to grow peaches. Two young college graduates, after hearing him speak, decided to try their fortunes at developing an orchard. When the man learned of their interest, he insisted that they allow him to help. He has worked hard with no financial reimbursement to teach those boys all he knows about growing peaches and to help them establish a producing orchard. His enthusiasm is contagious! He has found and given himself to a task that excites him and makes a valuable contribution to the welfare and health of others. He has chosen to live until he dies!

Growing older demands that we learn how to let go. We experience losses, sufferings, failures, and the death of others. Grief occurs over what we have lost or what has been taken from us. Some allow these losses to make them bitter, while others learn to relinquish what is gone and continue to appreciate that what they shared with another person or the meaning acquired from a certain thing is eternal. It has become a part of them.

The resources of the Christian faith can give us the attitude
Browning described when he wrote,

> Grow old along with me;
> The best is yet to be —
> The last of life for which the first was made.[4]

The greatest reason and resource for such an attitude is the One who
said, "And lo, I am with you all the days, — perpetually, uniformly
and on every occasion."[5]

Questions for Personal Reflection and Group Interaction

1. How do you feel about "growing older"?
2. Do you worship youth?
3. What age would you prefer to be, and why?
4. Can you recognize any new gifts that have come with age?
5. What kind of preparation are you making for aging?
6. Have you known an elderly person whose emotional and mental vigor inspired you? Did you recognize any attitudes in him that could account for his aliveness?
7. How flexible are you?
8. Have you learned how to gain perspective from your past?
9. Are you keeping in touch with your own unfolding story?
10. How do feel about your future? Why?
11. Are you ever bothered by self-pity?
12. Are you a complainer?
13. Are you investing yourself in something that really excites you?
14. How well have you learned to let go?
15. Can you celebrate the gift of life and the powers that are yours today?

27. Money Can Create Crises — When You Have It and When You Don't

MONEY HOLDS different meaning for different people. Depending on the values of the individual, it represents one or a combination of the following: *security, freedom, power, survival*. The availability of financial resources or the lack of them usually determines which of these is dominant.

Some view the acquisition of wealth as the prime goal of one's productivity, while others see it as the *means* for achieving some desired purpose in their future. More often than not it becomes the tangible yardstick for determining one's success or failure. Our materialistic system tends to make money synonymous with power and prestige: those who have it can exert greater influence in most circles than those who do not.

Materialistic values really determine how we spend or invest the resources at our disposal. We pay those who build our cars more than those who teach our children. We spend more on weapons for destruction than on humanitarian causes. The Christian has the distinctive assignment of being "salt and light" in the world in attempting to bring a more benevolent — thus godly — view to the use of our resources. We were made to *love people* and *use things*, but we can so easily become sidetracked and do the reverse.

The meaning we attach to our money determines the nature of our crisis, either when it is abundant or when we face a loss. Most of us would prefer the crises that come with abundance. However, the Bible indicates that the more difficult problems arise from affluence. Christ said to His disciples, "It is almost impossible for a rich man to get into the Kingdom of Heaven."[1]

Wealth tends to create a false security. Having the resources to do whatever one wishes is fun. But it can contribute to a haughty independence that ignores the need for God and makes one insensitive to the real needs of others. A sense of economic security is desirable for releasing a person to creative risk-taking in business; but alone it is inadequate for stimulating risk-taking in one's relationships.

What we really need is a deep sense of personal well-being that is not radically altered by either plenty or want. The Christian faith speaks distinctly to this need. Jesus Christ offers us a relationship based on unconditional love. Our response should be acceptance — acceptance of His gift. He becomes our constant companion with sufficient resources to enable us to experience the most and the best of life. If our money causes us to stumble and miss this gift, it becomes our curse. If our money is brought under His dominion, it becomes a blessed resource that can enrich our lives and all we touch with it.

I have seen money become both a curse and a blessing. Money is hard to manage properly without allowing it to dominate us or cause us to withdraw into selfish pleasures. But those who have given themselves and their resources to the living Christ have enabled others to pursue the mission Christ entrusted to them far beyond the limits of their economic resources. This is God's strategy — each member of Christ's body giving what he has the way Christ directs. The Lord then takes the bits and pieces that we offer and pulls the puzzle together in such a fashion as to create a positive, redemptive impact in the world.

Christian Concern Foundation — which employs ten of us as full- or part-time employees and operates Kaleo Lodge, a renewal center near Mineola in East Texas with a $100,000 budget — has for the past ten years had the financial resources needed with almost no promotion and scarcely any fund-raising activities. Fund-raising is not bad, but we have witnessed the potency of a small community of Christians giving their resources as they were led to enable a dream for ministry to emerge and endure. We have struggled in many ways, including the financial. The way has not always been easy. If it had, we would have missed some beautiful gifts from the Lord — gifts which caused us to recognize and celebrate His faithfulness and adequacy. Of course, we have never received a check signed by Jesus Christ to pay any bill; but He sent the resources through His people, enhancing the gift by including us as participants with Him in it.

Making partners of us is but one of the many amazing things about God's revelation of Himself and His action among men. He includes us as essential participants in His redemptive activity in history. He has a unique purpose for each of us that makes us, in a sense, indispensable. There is no one else like you, nor will there be; there is no one who can fill your place in the way God intends for you. We cannot thwart His ultimate purpose for history by our unresponsiveness to Him, but we can frustrate and nullify our part in it.

Periods of national economic stress, such as the recession of the mid-seventies, create for many persons financial crises unparalleled in their previous experience. Though an older generation remembers the Great Depression, the majority of persons in the thick of business and industry today do not. I have said that prosperity tends to create false security: well, it did! Not many years ago, few felt we could possibly have a serious recession, or one that would last any length of time. But in the recent recession, many businesses were stalled and some all but disappeared. Strangely enough, alongside the hard-hit industries, others experienced a boom. The mood in business circles remained cautious, if not pessimistic. A banker told me that customers making more money than ever were still pessimistic about the future.

An executive in one of the sharing groups I have been a part of has been unemployed for eight months; others whose incomes depend upon commissions and investments have not made a deal in a year. The repercussions from a situation like this can be devastating. I have observed, however, that men in these sharing groups have remained open and optimistic against bleak odds. I asked what enabled them to keep on and not give up in the face of such circumstances. The answers they gave me, along with their attitudes and responses to their predicament, convinced me again that the Christian faith does offer unique and indispensable resources for facing crises. It involved a struggle that at times threatened to overwhelm them. But to the Christian, the resources have been available for survival and for making something worthwhile out of the hardships themselves.

Let me share with you the resources those men discovered that made life rich in spite of and because of the difficult situations facing them.

1. The realization that God holds their destiny in His hands has enabled them to maintain a creative perspective. If a man believes he is alone in the universe with only blind fate operating, he has no place to turn for strength when his world crumbles, and he has no basis for any real hope. His struggle is robbed of any possible significance. But the biblical perspective of God's constant love and care, coupled with the freedom man has to make decisions that affect him and others deeply, opens the door to both understanding and hope.

Every man needs a faith to live by. As important as it is to believe in oneself, it does not enable us to survive when we reach the end of our rope. If coming to the end of ourselves (our resources and self-confidence) leads us to take that leap of faith (committing as much of ourselves as we can to as much of Jesus Christ as we understand), then the struggle has meaning and we will know we are not alone in it. That is good news, because it is the aloneness that breaks us far more than our losses.

2. When their perspective is clear, they know that the problems they are facing are really opportunities to test their resourcefulness and to build character. I said *when*, because these men who have become brothers to me are as human as any of us. Some days the battle gets to them, and they become discouraged. But they bounce back because they know there is a solution to their dilemma, even if

they do not see it today. They are unwilling to surrender to despair or to quit trying. The assignment that is theirs presents maximum opportunities to face themselves at a deeper level and to explore the resources of their faith.

Some may be skeptical and want to ask again, "Does a person's relationship to Jesus Christ really make any difference when the pressure is on?" Yes, it does! We will make mistakes. Yet I have seen these brothers of mine pass up several opportunities that could have alleviated the money crunch — at the expense of compromising themselves. "But remember this — the wrong desires that come into your life aren't anything new and different. Many others have faced exactly the same problems before you. And no temptation is irresistible. You can trust God to keep the temptation from becoming so strong that you can't stand up against it, for He has promised this and will do what He says. He will show you how to escape temptation's power so that you can bear up patiently against it."[2]

A life without tension is empty. If there were no problems to solve, no struggles to live through, no temptations to overcome, no doubts to resolve, no questions to answer, no differences of opinion to cope with, life would be motionless and we would be more like inanimate objects than human beings. It is these hard places, challenging and stretching us, that offer the greatest potential for discovery, growth, and character.

The resourcefulness that surfaced when these men were hard-pressed has been inspiring. The man who lost his job made his meager resources last, not the two months which he felt would be the longest they could possibly survive, but eight months. All the while he has aggressively pursued work. Between job interviews he has done appraisals and other short-term tasks. He has survived, and his openness to life and to other people has increased. Recently he called to inform me he had found a job after eight and a half months of looking. We celebrated!

Two men formerly in raw land syndication have moved into vegetable farming, and another who was in a brokerage company has moved into a challenging position in a large city bank. Still another, who had tried unsuccessfully the year before to move from law into real estate, found his law practice booming. He realizes now that a vocational change would have been disastrous for him financially.

These examples denote a lot of ferment for one small group. I learned that no matter how uncertain the way looks, if a man refuses to allow his situation to paralyze him and will rely on Christ, he will come through a better man, if not a richer one monetarily. "For every one who keeps on asking receives, and he who keeps on seeking finds, and to him who keeps on knocking it will be opened."[3]

3. These men accepted change when it was necessary. Sometimes we can be locked into our ideas and our position and block creative alternatives for solving our dilemma. For a person to think there is only one solution creates fear and blinds him to both potential within and opportunities without. Change can be painful, because it is risky. But it can also be very stimulating as we accept a new challenge that demands the acquisition of additional information and offers new relationships and tasks. Beginning a new career can be, and often is, fun!

4. These men also sought the counsel of others whose wisdom and experience were essential assets as they explored different possibilities. Someone has said, "Experience is a hard school, but a fool will learn in no other." There are people who can help us if we will but ask. Something as important as the field in which a man will invest himself vocationally should be considered with others who are knowledgeable in it. The writer of Proverbs says, "Plans go wrong with too few counselors; many counselors bring success."[4] There is great advantage in getting many different viewpoints before you make your decision.

5. Live within your means. One of the men in the sharing group told me, "I had to change my spending habits." He asked himself two questions when it came to spending money: (a) do I really need it?; and (b) can I afford it? It's easy to move up the ladder in the matter of spending, but scaling down comes hard.

6. Take it one day at a time. Another of the men considered this absolutely essential for him. There were plenty of problems in any given day to keep him busy, and when he allowed projected problems from the future to crowd into the present, his anxiety grew too great. Christ said, "Don't be anxious about tomorrow. God will

take care of your tomorrow too. Live one day at a time."[5]

7. Hang on to the belief that one day the light will break. It may not come as soon as we want or even the way we want, but it will come. It may change our life-style and cause us to use the resources we have with less waste. It may alter our values radically so that we are less materialistic and more concerned with God's purpose and human need. We may learn how to travel lighter as pilgrims of faith, or we may be given the responsibility of managing greater wealth for the good of all.

Remember that in the midst of your severest struggle, God is up to something! He has no desire to hurt you, but to help you discover yourself, Him, and your place in His purpose. He loves you and shares the agony and the ecstasy with you.

Questions for Personal Reflection and Group Interaction

1. What meaning does money have for you — what does it represent to you or promise you?
2. On a scale from 0 to 10, what number do you think best represents your ability to manage money?
3. How can wealth create false security? Has it ever done so for you?
4. From what sources do you gain your security?
5. What determines whether money will be a blessing or a curse?
6. Have you ever been in a situation where you lost your financial resources or thought you would? What were your feelings and reactions? How did you cope with the pressure? Did you grieve over your loss? Have you fully recovered emotionally, regardless of the finances?
7. Are you a loner or an individualist who feels that it's all up to you to make it — no one else can or will help? Or are you one who feels that others will or should help you make it financially or otherwise?
8. Have you discovered within your Christian faith the resources, not only for survival, but for making something worthwhile out of your hardships? What, or how?
9. Do financial problems tend to paralyze you, or challenge you?
10. Have you learned to live within your means?
11. If you could make a simple plan enabling you to use your economic resources creatively and wisely, what do you think would be included? Why not try it?

28. Resources for the Journey Through Our Crises

OF THE MANY THINGS that the Christian faith is not, it is not immunity from pain or struggle or from any one of the many calamities that life sometimes brings. Christ did not come to eliminate all crises, but to enable us to move through the hard places in a manner that deepens life and, yes, even enriches it. He frees us to face reality, not to hide from it. But His promise to us is "I am with you. . . ."[1] It is His presence that makes the real difference and enables us to believe that our tragedies are not senseless. He can work redemptively in even our most devastating experience.

Elisabeth Elliot, who lost her first husband at the hands of the Auca Indians in 1956, tells in her book, A *Slow and Certain Light*, the story of two young adventurers who came to see her. She was in Ecuador, and these two young men were on their way to the rain forest east of the Andes. They had all kinds of equipment, most of it more cumbersome than helpful. They did not want her evaluation of their supplies nor advice about their trip. All they wanted were a few phrases of the Indian language. They were certain this was all they lacked to be fully prepared for their journey. Elisabeth Elliot writes:

> Sometimes we come to God as the two adventurers came to me — confident and, we think, well-informed and well-equipped. But it has occurred to us that with all our accumulation of stuff something is missing. There is just one thing we will have to ask God for, and we hope He will not find it necessary to sort through the other things. There's nothing there that we're willing to do without. We know what we need — a yes or no answer, please, to a simple question. Or perhaps a road sign. Something quick and easy to point the way.
>
> What we really ought to have is the Guide himself. Maps, road signs, a few useful phrases are good things, but infinitely better is someone who has been there before and knows the way.[2]

The greatest resource of the Christian faith is just such a Guide. Jesus Christ has been there ahead of us. He knows the way; He understands the pain and, what's more, He offers to walk with us through it all. More often than not, *the struggle does not break us, but rather our sense of aloneness in it.* It is this "aloneness" Christ attacks first. Once He has our attention, and we know that in spite of all our fears and negative feelings He is with us, we can begin to cope creatively with our crisis. *Hope* enters the picture, and with it comes the *will* to keep on fighting the good fight.

Having the right answers, as important as that is, becomes secondary to having a right relationship with Jesus Christ. He enables you to live in the midst of the storm far better than the resources your sight or strength could ever provide.

Seek the greatest gift first. Ask the living Christ to come into your life, to forgive you and heal you of your hopelessness. Ask Him to help you put the pieces of your life back together — but His way this time. Then begin to take responsible steps such as the ones suggested in this section. It may not be quick and easy, but it will be real and life-changing.

In each chapter I have tried to relate practical ways Christ works to change our attitudes and our situations. These are by no means exhaustive, merely suggestive. There is, however, one other matter I want to share with you, which is one of the great gifts of the gospel — *the freedom to fail.* Fear of failure can be paralyzing. It can create undue caution that may actually keep us from experiencing real success.

The powerful ending to the story of Zorba the Greek beautifully illustrates this freedom to fail. Zorba has all the bossman's money invested in building an apparatus to bring timber down the mountain to the community to be used to reinforce the walls of the old mine. Excitement fills the air! Opening the mine will restore economic life to that little Greek village, and everyone is on hand to watch and celebrate this great occasion. But all hopes are dashed when the huge logs cause the slide to collapse. The villagers leave in despair.

Only Zorba and the bossman stay. After cutting off a slice of meat, Zorba sits down beside the bossman and they begin to talk. The bossman speaks dejectedly about leaving the village, but holds out a half-hearted "maybe we will meet again." Zorba says no. He knows this is their final visit, and he is willing to face that reality, even if it hurts. Then Zorba says, "Bossman, I have never loved a man as I have loved you, but there is one thing you lack: a little madness to be free."

The bossman, who all along has been amazed by Zorba's ability to live life so full, just looks at him. Zorba stands up, looks at the crumbled log slide, and begins to laugh.

"Why are you laughing?" asks the bossman.

Zorba replies, "Have you ever seen a more stupendous crash in your life?"

The bossman responds with, "Zorba, will you teach me to dance?" And the story closes with the two men dancing and celebrating life at the site of their greatest failure.

Only Christ can do that for real in us. He enables us to separate ourselves from our projects. For we are more than our projects. What we do has temporary value in many respects: it will pass away. But what we become is eternal. Christ offers Himself as our security base. Once we realize that our lives are "safe" in Him, in the highest sense of that word, we can begin to view our projects with some objectivity and know that the destruction of our work can be a learning, growing experience that may even launch us into a greater task. The *freedom to fail* allows the kind of freedom essential for success to blossom. Learn to celebrate life, the bitter with the sweet, in the company of Christ.

Questions for Personal Reflection and Group Interaction

1. Have you ever felt that you were utterly alone in your struggles?
2. Have you ever invited the living Christ to come into your life and put the pieces of your life together His way? If so, what has happened? If not, why?
3. Have you rejected or accepted a tradition or caricature of Christianity? Do you know the basic message of the Christian faith? What has God offered us in Jesus Christ? How do we appropriate, or receive, His gift? Have you ever committed your life to Him?
4. Do you operate under the fear of failure?
5. Have you ever experienced the *freedom to fail*, discussed in this chapter? Did that freedom enable you to do a better job with the tasks at hand?

PART FOUR

Facing the Ultimate Crisis — Death

Lord, help me to realize how brief my time on earth will be. Help me to know that I am here for but a moment more. My life is no longer than my hand! My whole lifetime is but a moment to you. Proud man! Frail as breath! A shadow! And all his busy rushing ends in nothing. He heaps up riches for someone else to spend. And so, Lord, my only hope is in you.

— Psalm 39:4-7
The Living Bible

amen .

29. Facing Our Own Death

WE HAVE ALL HEARD someone say, "I am not afraid of death." The person making such a statement, in all probability, was not facing death at that moment. It is always easier to be heroic in our fantasies than in reality. Death can be a grim and frightening experience, especially for those who have never really come to terms with their finitude or have not found an adequate faith for dying.

To make matters worse, we live in a society bent on ignoring or avoiding death. We want to keep the dying isolated, and we want to see the dead only when they have been dressed to look "natural" — which really means to look as if they are still alive. We try to keep our children away from such morbid reality by telling them stories and sending them away until everything is over.

The truth is that, with a little help, our children can understand and cope with this reality better than we. Facing the death of another person can have a redemptive impact upon us. It is a reality we all will experience. We are born, we live, we die. That is the drama of all living things, including man. To whatever extent we are out of touch with this fact, we are out of touch with reality.

The realization that we, too, will die makes life even more precious. It is not to be wasted; it is not unlimited; we have a deadline beyond which we cannot go. Emotionally this reality is almost impossible to grasp. We have less difficulty believing that others die, but we hang onto the illusion that life will go on for us on this earth always. It usually takes some shattering experience to drive home the reality that we are mortal.

One man said, "We are not ready to live until we come to terms with our own death." It is in facing not only the possibility of our death but its inevitability that we are driven to seek out the meaning of our life. Life must have meaning, else death has no significance. We can rest assured that we will die as we have lived — fearful, vain, cantankerous, or honest, trusting, purposeful.

An awareness of our limits can help us to get our priorities straight. What is of real value to you? How would you spend your energy and time if you knew you had three months or six months or one year to live? Why don't you spend yourself that way, even without a specific deadline?

Facing the actuality of death gives spiritual realities top priority. If God is, we know we need Him now. We may have spent a lifetime running away from the reality that we did not born ourselves and owe our very existence to the God who created us. In facing death which is before us, we cannot escape the reality that our destiny is in His hands. Just as God has been present with us in life — whether we recognized Him or not — He is present with us in death. God has, in the life, death, and resurrection of His Son, Jesus Christ, conquered death. He will conquer death in us if we will but open our lives to Him. To open your life, pray this simple prayer and mean it:

> Lord Jesus, I am a needy creature. I have lived my life as I pleased, and now I repent of all the follies of my self-centeredness. I ask you to forgive me, to accept me into your family, and to give me the grace to live and to die with dignity.

Sometimes death comes quickly, and sometimes it lingers. When death lingers and it becomes our lot to go through great suffering prior to our demise, then we can expect to move through different stages and attitudes toward this reality.[1]

The first reaction we can expect when we become aware that our illness is terminal is denial. Impending death comes as a shock. "This could not be happening to me; it can't be true; I have so much to do yet; it's a mistake." These feelings leave us numb. Elisabeth Kübler-Ross states, "Denial functions as a buffer after unexpected shocking news, allows the patient to collect himself and, with time, mobilize other, less radical defenses."[2] Denial may also be used from time to time throughout the duration of one's illness for emotional relief. This is both normal and healthy.

2. The second stage may be anger. The question that may express some of our anger is, "Why me? Why should others be young and healthy and strong and live, and I have to die?" This resentment is hard for others to understand or manage, because it goes in all directions without apparent reason. If we could place ourselves in the shoes of one dying, we might understand. "Maybe we too would be angry if all our life activities were interrupted so prematurely; if all the buildings we started were to go unfinished, to be completed by someone else; if we had put some hard-earned money aside to enjoy a few years of rest and enjoyment, for travel and pursuing hobbies, only to be confronted with the fact that 'this is not for me.'"[3]

Facing death is a tough assignment. But God gives us permission to work through these negative emotions, and we should grant the same permission to those we love. Perhaps it will be easier if we understand that this is only a part of the process as one moves toward accepting death.

3. The third stage may be an attempt to bargain our way out of the situation. If our anger has not helped, perhaps God will be more inclined to save us from death if we ask nicely. Attempting to postpone the inevitable, we may make all kinds of promises to God. If we discover that God has given us more time, we can celebrate and make the most of it — but we must face the reality that there will not be a permanent postponement.

4. Depression is also a common stage through which many pass as they face death. Kübler-Ross points out that there are two stages of depression, and they must be dealt with differently. The first has to do with past loss — loss of health, loss of control of one's own life, loss of job or finances, loss of dreams and plans, loss of one's

ability to function and meet the needs of those dependent upon him. Alleviating any unrealistic guilt or shame with positive, affirmative statements to cheer him up may help the person greatly.

The second stage of depression may arise when the individual contemplates his impending loss. Trying to cheer him up by telling him to look on the brighter side will only get in the way of the process. The truth is, he is preparing for the loss of everyone and everything he loves.

If he is allowed to express his sorrow he will find a final acceptance much easier, and he will be grateful to those who can sit with him during this state of depression without constantly telling him not to be sad. This second type of depression is usually a silent one in contrast to the first type, during which the patient has much to share and requires many verbal interactions. . . . In the preparatory grief there is no or little need for words. It is much more a feeling that can be mutually expressed and is often done better with a touch of a hand, a stroking of the hair, or just a silent sitting together. This is the time when the patient may just ask for a prayer, when he begins to occupy himself with things ahead rather than behind. It is a time when too much interference from visitors who try to cheer him up hinders his emotional preparation rather than enhances it.[4]

5. The final stage is acceptance. If a person is allowed to work through the anguish and anxiety that inevitably accompany the imminence of death, he will be able to accept his situation with a degree of quiet expectancy.

Acceptance should not be mistaken for a happy stage. It is almost void of feelings. It is as if the pain had gone, the struggle is over, and there comes a time for "the final rest before the long journey" as one patient phrased it. This is also the time during which the family needs usually more help, understanding, and support than the patient himself. While the dying patient has found some peace and acceptance, his circle of interest diminishes. He wishes to be left alone or at least not stirred up by news and problems of the outside world.[5]

Obviously not every terminally ill person passes through these exact stages. But we should be aware of the process through which we will pass to one degree or another in facing our own or a loved one's death.

Paramount for all of us at all times is *a need to be treated as a person rather than as an object*. This is never clearer than when we are seriously ill or dying. Sometimes loved ones, doctors, and nurses may be so intent on "helping" us or attending us that they overlook our need to be included in decision making. Each person has the right to participate in his treatment as a thinking, deciding human being as long as he can function as such.

A man must be given the right to die with dignity. Should he choose to die rather than to vegetate, his choice should be respected by the medical profession, the laws of the land, and the family.

As already mentioned, the way we have lived, the person that we have become, is more determinative than anything else in the way we will face our death. A good friend, Mickey Warlick, has battled a malignant brain tumor for more than five years. He has a lovely wife and two beautiful children. He is thirty-five years old — young, with so much to live for! Mickey underwent several operations, but recently we learned that the cancer is growing again.

Five years ago the doctor gave Mickey at best a few months to live. He and Shirley have lived under the shadow of death for five years, but they are living richly. A year ago I flew out to see them because I wanted to say, "We love you both!" What I saw, felt, and heard blessed me beyond words. Two people, deeply in love with each other, with life, and with Jesus Christ, gave such an authentic witness to the reality of God's sustaining grace that had I been an unbeliever, I would have believed! Mickey's attitude is "I am going to live until I die!"

A thought went through my mind then, as it does today: how many of us quit living long before we die? We cease to dream or to change or to risk new frontiers. God calls us to life, and Mickey has responded as wholeheartedly to that call as any man I know. His faith has made extraordinary resources available for his journey. The biblical models of how other men faced great difficulties and even death — how they overcame their fear and were able by God's power to make the life they had count for good — has opened the door for Mickey to walk in the Way. Mickey is making steps uniquely his own through which God is pointing the way for many of the rest of us.

Mickey and Shirley's experience bears witness to the biblical reality that God will give us grace to live and grace to die as we need it. We can trust Him even beyond our understanding.

Mickey believes, and the Bible teaches, that death for a believer in Christ is but a new and glorious beginning. Such a concept changes the shape of our future from facing death as a loss to facing it as an adventure. We step out of this life with all its limitations, struggles, and questions into the very presence of the living God. We shall know and understand just as we have been known and understood by God Himself. The Scriptures declare, "Eye hath not seen, nor ear heard, neither have entered into the heart of man, the things which God hath prepared for them that love Him."[6]

God's gift to us is beyond our wildest dreams! One biblical example reads, "And the street of the city was pure gold, as it were transparent glass."[7] What men count of highest value in this world is used to pave the streets there. And another, "There shall be no night there; and they need no candle, neither light of the sun; for the Lord God giveth them light: and they shall reign for ever and ever."[8]

Christ conquered death, and He can conquer it in us if we will but open our lives to Him. He says to us, as we confront some part of life or death that we cannot handle, "Peace I leave with you, my peace I give unto you: not as the world giveth, give I unto you. Let not your heart be troubled, neither let it be afraid. . . . I will not leave you comfortless: I will come unto you."[9]

Questions for Personal Reflection and Group Interaction

1. Do you fear death?
2. Have you ever thought seriously about the fact that one day death will come to you? What caused you to face this reality? Or why haven't you faced this reality?
3. How can coming to grips with our own death help us to live more fully?
4. What does death mean to you?
5. Have you ever worked with or stood by someone who was in the process of dying? Can you recognize any of the stages through which they were passing, as mentioned in this chapter?
6. How can you best help a terminally ill person?
7. What unique resource does the Christian message bring to one facing death?

30. The Crisis of Grief

GRIEF IS THE RESPONSE of emotional pain to great loss. To lose anyone or anything of real significance produces grief. The loss may occur as a result of death, divorce, children's leaving home, moving; from the loss of a job, of reputation, security, money, or one of the senses, such as sight. We need to remember that the greater the emotional investment in the person or object lost, the more intense the pain. For our purposes here we focus on death; but the same reactions can be observed in other grief-filled situations.

Our family has experienced grief recently. My wife lost her father; her mother, her husband; our children, their grandfather; and I, a friend and father-in-law. Events still occur that cause me to experience waves of emotion. These feelings were triggered as I worked on some wiring that Eldred helped me with shortly before his death. The vivid memory of our work together brought to the surface again my sense of loss. And with this sense of loss came also real gratitude for what he had given me.

I became aware that the healing process was at work. Joy

and sorrow are mixed. I know that none of us will ever be quite the same; but we can be more than we have been because he lived and loved and touched us deeply by both his life and his death. One vivid example is what David, our then thirteen-year-old son, wrote regarding the loss of his grandfather.

I see an oak upon a hill
I see the sun behind it still.

I see a grave in all its fame.
We loved the man behind the name.

I see a star way up above.
I sense the Lord and feel his love.

I hear a breeze and know for sure
that now, my granddad is really pure.

I see a sunset in the sky;
I see a rainbow start to die;
I watch the river softly flow;
I feel the wind begin to blow.

There is a love so deep inside,
It's very hard for me to hide.

But I'm not scared to wake at dawn.
The Lord has called and he has gone.

I know it's best for everyone
to remember the good and remember the fun.

But there's something else I seem to feel —
something strong, something real.

I know not yet what it might be.
It could be fear, or maybe just me.

But whatever it is, it really pains;
It hurts much more than a fiery rain.

If I could explain it, then you might know,
But it's even too hard for me to show.

It's something new and different to touch,
It burns and hurts so very much.

But deep inside I know it's love;
A love that will not die.
A love that someone gives or takes;
Not one that you can buy!

So as I watch the sun go down
behind my memory hill,
I think of all the love there is
within our family still.

It takes time for the wound to heal. But the healing can make us stronger, more sensitive, and appreciative of life and of the people who love us.

Let us turn our attention to the different reactions we will, in all probability, experience in grief. The first is *shock*: "How can this be?" It will seem unreal. It's hard to register the reality of the loss. We will be numb and may appear dazed, confused, or stoic. We simply need a little time at this stage for the reality of our situation to sink in.

Emotional release usually follows the shock. It is not "Christian" to choke back the tears. The great men of faith wept over loss, and so did the Lord Himself. It is healthy and needful to cry. Give your feelings expression! Healing comes faster when you do.

Feelings of hostility and guilt may be present in our grief. It hurts so bad that we may become very critical of everyone and everything related to our loss. This may include the doctors and nurses, family members, and even God Himself. "Why would God permit such a thing to happen?" we often ask. While we may not find an adequate explanation, we can know a God who cares for us so deeply that He too participates in our suffering. He allows us to work through our hostile feelings without rejecting us or withdrawing His love. One indication that we have worked through our grief is the realization that we can trust God beyond our understanding of Him or the events of life.

Guilt is a painful part of grief. "Why didn't we do more? Why did we do some of the things we did?" The tendency is to distort reality. We need to remember that we may be reading too much out of our present grief reaction back into our prior relationship with the deceased.

The mistakes we made can be faced and committed to the living Christ. His forgiveness is readily available. Now the tough task of forgiving ourselves must be undertaken for freedom to come.

Depression and withdrawal are common to the grief process. We may feel that no one else has ever grieved as we are grieving, and that no one really cares, not even God. It is dark; all hope seems to disappear. Recognizing this as a normal part of our dealing with grief can keep us from becoming panic-stricken over what is to become of us. This too will pass — if we let it!

6   *Great loneliness and the loss of meaning* are common and normal. The people we love are a vital part of us. When they die, a part of us dies too. What seemed important before may lose its importance, and we are left with a sense of emptiness. The person we intended to share our life with continually is gone, and no one can take his place. The loneliness will seem unbearable! But others have experienced the same and have survived. You can survive too. Even Christ experienced the agony of aloneness on the cross when He cried out, "My God, my God, why hast thou forsaken me?"[1] Jesus has promised to be present with us and never to leave us comfortless. He does not take the place of another person in our lives: no one can. But He can take His own place as Lord and bring unbelievable resources into our lives to heal and even give our loss meaning.

7   *Anxiety and fear* are also normal. "What am I going to do?" becomes a focal question. We may have never considered life without the one we lost. For a time we will be disoriented. This is normal, because facing the unknown always creates its share of anxiety. Fear also relates to the future dimension of grief. The death of someone close makes us keenly aware of the fact that we too will die.

There are some definite steps we can take to bring about healing in our times of grief. First, *we need to express our emotions.* Holding everything in only hinders our recovery. Talking with a family member, a friend, or a minister about both our negative and positive feelings will do wonders for us. As already mentioned, there may be feelings of anger, guilt, anxiety, or fear. Talking about these feelings diminishes them and serves as a kind of confession that opens the way for the positive feelings of love and gratitude, even joy, to return.

It helps to talk about the deceased, to recall events experienced with him. This helps you face the reality of your loss, release your emotions, and affirm the life of the deceased, whose influence and contribution to your own life will never die. The memory of the deceased will remain and even enrich your life further as you learn to let them go.

Verdell's mother did a beautiful thing prior to her husband's funeral. She gathered her children and their spouses around the casket and talked openly of her great loss. Then she prayed and gave thanks for the forty rich years they had together. The final act of her prayer was to give him up to God. She later said that in that moment she experienced a "letting go" of Eldred. It's hard, but we must let go of the person if we are to experience healing. It takes time to turn loose, but if we are moving in that direction, we can count on the resources of the living Christ to enable us to allow our beloved to rest in peace.

Death can make us aware of the unlimited resources of faith in a way that nothing else can. To be without a solid faith in Jesus Christ is to find death the loneliest experience of life. With Christ we discover the truth of His statement, "I will not leave you comfortless: I will come to you."[2] This does not mean that there will be no pain or struggle. It does mean that nowhere in all the world is the pain felt as keenly and as deeply as it is in the heart of God. He is in it with us and will help us when no one else can.

A relationship with Christ brings hope, and without hope we would all die in despair. This world is not the whole story. There is life beyond death, and the prospect of being reunited someday with the one we have lost brings joy indeed. The older we get, the more we should realize that the balance of our investment is shifting from this world to the next. This realization will not only help us accept the loss of a loved one, but will lessen the anxiety and fear in facing our own death.

Finally, give yourself some time for the wound to heal. Don't push yourself too fast. In the death of your beloved, you have lost a significant person who was an important part of your life. It takes time to recuperate, and the amount of time varies with the individual. It is imperative that each person work through his own anguish completely.

Unresolved grief is destructive. Therefore deal honestly with your feelings; allow others to walk with you in your sorrow; hold firmly to your faith in the God whose death and life can enable you to move beyond every loss into the fuller hope that is yours in Him. Then you will know the meaning of the Scripture, "Grieve not as those who have no hope."[3]

Questions for Personal Reflection
and Group Interaction

1. Have you ever experienced a loss that created a deep sense of grief? What was it?
2. How did you express your grief?
3. Were you able to work through your grief, or do you feel that some of it may still be bottled up inside?
4. Did you experience any feelings of hostility or guilt; depression; loss of meaning or great loneliness; anxiety? What did you do with these feelings?
5. What positive things did you discover or experience out of your loss and grief?
6. Were you able to give yourself time for the wound to heal, or did you panic, thinking that it would never be better?
7. From what source did you find the hope that enabled you to move ahead?
8. Do you know anyone personally who is now going through a time of grief? How do you think you can help?

Notes

(Key to abbreviations: LB = *The Living Bible*; Amp. = *The Amplified Bible*; RSV = *Revised Standard Version*; KJV = *King James Version*.)

CHAPTER 1 — HOW DO YOU REACT TO CONFLICT?
The epigraph is from *I Ain't Much, Baby — But I'm All I've Got* by Jess Lair. Garden City, N.Y.: Doubleday & Company, 1972, p. 199.

CHAPTER 2 — CREATIVE RELATIONSHIPS DO NOT HAPPEN ACCIDENTALLY
1. James 2:1, RSV
2. Romans 2:11, New English Bible
3. Galatians 3:26, 28, Phillips
4. Francis A. Schaeffer. *No Little People*. Downers Grove, Ill.: Inter-Varsity Press, 1974, pp. 13, 20.
5. Maxie Dunnam. *Be Your Whole Self*. Atlanta, Ga.: Forum House, Inc., 1970, p. 85.
6. 1 John
7. 1 Corinthians 13:4-7, LB; 8a, Amp.

CHAPTER 4 — SUBSTITUTES FOR INTIMACY
1. Leviticus 26:8, 12, LB
2. Leviticus 26:17, LB

3. Howard J. and Charlotte H. Clinebell. *The Intimate Marriage.* New York: Harper & Row, 1970, p. 56.
4. Matthew 23:3b-5a, LB
5. Matthew 18:2, 3, LB

CHAPTER 5 — MANAGING YOUR EMOTIONS
1. Dietrich Bonhoeffer. *Life Together.* New York: Harper & Row, 1954, pp. 27-28.
2. For further examination of how to deal with these strong emotions in an intimate relationship, see *The Intimate Marriage* by Clinebell and Clinebell; *The Becomers* by Keith Miller; and *Search for Silence* by Elizabeth O'Connor.
3. John 15:12, KJV
4. Matthew 23
5. Matthew 16:23
6. Matthew 21:12, 13
7. Matthew 18:6
8. Matthew 7:1-5, RSV
9. Karl A. Menninger. *The Human Mind.* New York: The Literary Guild of America, 1933, p. 33; as quoted in *Our Many Selves* by Elizabeth O'Connor. New York: Harper & Row, 1971, p. 86.

CHAPTER 6 — KEEPING THE LINES OF COMMUNICATION OPEN
1. Virginia Satir. *Peoplemaking.* Palo Alto, Calif.: Science & Behavior Books, Inc., 1972, p. 59.
2. Ibid., p. 77.

CHAPTER 7 — YOUR SENSE OF HUMOR — A VALUABLE ASSET
1. Elton Trueblood. *The Humor of Christ.* New York: Harper & Row, 1964, p. 55.
2. John 16:33b, RSV

CHAPTER 8 — PRAYER — A NEGLECTED RESOURCE
1. Luke 18:10-14, KJV
2. Isaiah 40:31, KJV
3. Joshua 24:15b, paraphrased
4. Matthew 5:44c, KJV
5. Matthew 5:9, KJV

CHAPTER 9 — FORGIVENESS — AN ESSENTIAL INGREDIENT
1. Karl Menninger. *Whatever Became of Sin?* New York: Hawthorn Books, 1973, p. 17.
2. 2 Corinthians 5:17, LB
3. Psalm 32:1-5, LB
4. Galatians 6:7b, KJV
5. Luke 19:8, LB
6. Mark 11:25, RSV
7. Matthew 23:2-5b, 13, LB

CHAPTER 10 — WORKING WITH SOMEONE YOU DON'T LIKE
    1. Philippians 2:13, LB

CHAPTER 11 — LIVING WITH AN ALCOHOLIC
    1. Pastor Paul. *The 13th American*. Elgin, Ill.: David C. Cook Publishing Co., 1973, pp. 71-72.
    2. For the purpose of readability only, we will refer to the alcoholic in masculine terms. Statistically, more than 30 percent of this nation's alcoholics are women. Experts refer to this known 30 percent as "the tip of the iceberg," because so many female alcoholics are hidden at home by their families, too ignorant or ashamed to obtain for them the help they so desperately need. We also do not intend to ignore, by inference or example, the adolescent alcoholic. Statistics clearly show that the most dramatic rise in alcoholism is occurring during the teen-age years.
    3. Pastor Paul, *The 13th American*, pp. 105-6.
    4. Ibid., p. 106.
    5. Howard J. Clinebell, Jr. *Understanding and Counseling the Alcoholic*. New York: Abingdon Press, 1956, p. 19.
    6. *Alcoholics Anonymous*. New York: Alcoholics Anonymous World Services, Inc., 2nd ed., 1955, p. 31.
    7. Marty Mann. *Primer on Alcoholism*. Pages 172-73: as quoted in Clinebell, *Understanding and Counseling the Alcoholic*, p. 242.
    8. Carroll A. Wise. *Religion in Illness and Health*. New York: Harper Brothers, 1942, p. 37.
    9. Pastor Paul, *The 13th American*, pp. 154-55.
    10. *Alcoholics Anonymous*, pp. 59-60.
    11. *Alcoholism — The Family Disease*. Pamphlet. New York: Al-Anon Family Group Headquarters, Inc., 1972, p. 4.

CHAPTER 12 — COPING WITH EMOTIONAL DISTURBANCES
    1. Isaiah 55:8, 9, LB
    2. Proverbs 12:15, KJV
    3. John 9:2, 3a, LB

CHAPTER 13 — SINGLE AND UNCERTAIN?
    1. 1 Corinthians 7:17, LB
    2. From pp. 2-5 in *I Loved a Girl* by Walter Trobisch. Copyright © 1963, 1964 by Walter Trobisch. By permission of Harper & Row, Publishers, Inc.
    3. Gini Andrews. *Your Half of the Apple*. Grand Rapids: Zondervan Publishing House, 1972, p. 85.
    4. John 8:11, KJV

CHAPTER 14 — CONFLICT BETWEEN PARENTS AND ADOLESCENTS
    1. Ephesians 6:1-3, LB

CHAPTER 15 — CONFLICT WITH PARENTS AND IN-LAWS
    1. I am assuming here that the couple is happily married. If one or the other spouse is acting cruelly or irresponsibly, then the feelings of a

parent may be justified, because they are based on reality and not on resentment.
2. Genesis 2:24, KJV

CHAPTER 16 — LIVING BEYOND OUR FAILURES
1. John 1:10-12, KJV
2. Luke 17:33, LB

CHAPTER 17 — WHERE DID IT ALL BEGIN?
1. Job 14:1, 2, LB
2. For those interested in a fuller explanation of God's magnificent purpose, see my book *Beyond This God Cannot Go*. Grand Rapids: Zondervan Publishing House, 1971. See especially chapter 6, "More Than I Expected."
3. Romans 8:17, LB
4. Romans 5:1-5a, LB
5. 2 Corinthians 11:24-29, LB

CHAPTER 18 — NO ONE IS EXEMPT
1. Proverbs 13:15b, KJV
2. Psalm 73:2-5, 7-8, 13-14, 16, LB
3. Psalm 73:18-20, LB
4. 1 Corinthians 15:19, LB
5. Romans 8:18, RSV
6. 1 Corinthians 2:9, KJV
7. James 1:17a, LB
8. Matthew 5:44, 45, LB
9. Moral evil is the havoc wrought by evil desires and deeds. Natural evil is the ugliness, pain, frustration, and death caused by disease and natural disasters beyond human control.

CHAPTER 19 — WHEN IT RAINS, IT POURS!
1. Thomas Holmes. "Your Emotional Stress Can Make You Sick." *Chicago Tribune*, 18 July 1972, sec. 1, pp. 1ff.: as quoted in *How to Win Over Depression* by Tim LaHaye. Grand Rapids: Zondervan Publishing House, 1974, pp. 107-8.
2. LaHaye, *How to Win Over Depression*, p. 109.
3. Ibid., p. 111.
4. John 14:18, LB

CHAPTER 20 — THE GOSPEL OF SUCCESS vs. THE GOSPEL OF REDEMPTION
1. John 6:26, LB
2. John 6:60b, RSV
3. John 6:66, RSV
4. John 6:68, 69, RSV
5. Luke 10:20, RSV
6. C. William Fisher. *Don't Park Here!* New York: Abingdon Press, 1962, pp. 42-43.

CHAPTER 21 — HOW DO YOU HANDLE YOUR CRISES ?
1. Job 1:21, KJV
2. Job 2:4, 5
3. Job 2:9, RSV
4. Job 2:10, paraphrased
5. Job 42:5, KJV
6. Exodus 34:8, KJV

CHAPTER 22 — COPING WITH SENSELESS TRAGEDY
1. Psalm 38:8-11, LB
2. Viktor E. Frankl. *Man's Search for Meaning.* New York: Pocket Books, 1959, pp. 104-5.
3. Psalm 46:1-11, LB
4. Romans 8:28, RSV
5. Hebrews 11:10, Amp.

CHAPTER 23 — THE LOSS OF MEANING
1. Viktor E. Frankl. *Man's Search for Meaning.* New York: Pocket Books, 1959, p. 121.
2. Ibid., pp. 205-6.
3. Hebrews 11:24, 25, LB
4. I consider God's redemptive purpose in more detail in chapter 6, "More Than I Expected," in my book *Beyond This God Cannot Go.* Grand Rapids: Zondervan Publishing House, 1971.

CHAPTER 24 — RECOVERING FROM A MORAL FAILURE
1. Hosea 8:7
2. For a fuller explanation of the wisdom of God revealed in the ethics of the Judeo-Christian faith, see Chapter 6, "An Adequate Value System," in my book *Sent to Be Vulnerable.* Grand Rapids: Zondervan Publishing House, 1973.

CHAPTER 25 — PAIN AND SUFFERING
1. 1 Samuel 12:22a, KJV
2. Viktor E. Frankl. *Man's Search for Meaning.* New York: Pocket Books, 1959, pp. 123-24.
3. Iona Henry and Frank S. Mead. *Triumph Over Tragedy.* Westwood, N.J.: Fleming H. Revell Co., 1957, pp. 49, 77-78: as quoted in *Don't Park Here!* by C. William Fisher. New York: Abingdon Press, 1962, p. 89.
4. From *Guideposts to a Stronger Faith.* Ed. by Norman Vincent Peale. Copyright 1956 by Guideposts Associates, Inc. Published at Carmel, New York. Pages 175-80, used by permission of George B. Lieberman and quoted in *Don't Park Here!* by C. William Fisher. New York: Abingdon Press, 1962, p. 90.

CHAPTER 26 — WE ARE ALL GROWING OLDER
1. Job 12:12, 13, LB
2. James 1:5, LB

3. Reuel L. Howe. *How to Stay Young While Growing Older*. Waco, Tex.: Word Books, 1974, pp. 142, 144.
4. *Leaves of Gold*. Ed. by Clyde Francis Lytle. Pennsylvania: The Coslett Publishing Co., rev. ed., 1957, p. 5.
5. Matthew 28:20b, Amp.

CHAPTER 27 — MONEY CAN CREATE CRISES — WHEN YOU HAVE IT AND WHEN YOU DON'T
1. Matthew 19:23, LB
2. 1 Corinthians 10:13, LB
3. Matthew 7:8, Amp.
4. Proverbs 15:22, LB
5. Matthew 6:34, LB

CHAPTER 28 — RESOURCES FOR THE JOURNEY THROUGH OUR CRISES
1. Matthew 28:20
2. Elisabeth Elliot. *A Slow and Certain Light*. Waco, Tex.: Word Books, 1973, p. 20.

CHAPTER 29 — FACING OUR OWN DEATH
1. Elisabeth Kübler-Ross, medical director of the Family Service and Mental Health Center of South Cook County, Illinois, has brought most helpful insight from her work with dying patients to our attention in her book *On Death and Dying* (New York: Macmillan Co., 1969). It is from her work that I have derived the five stages through which a terminally ill patient may pass.
2. Elisabeth Kübler-Ross. *On Death and Dying*. New York: Macmillan Co., 1969, p. 39.
3. Ibid., p. 51.
4. Ibid., pp. 87-88.
5. Ibid., p. 113.
6. 1 Corinthians 2:9, KJV
7. Revelation 21:21, KJV
8. Revelation 22:5, KJV
9. John 14:27, 18, KJV

CHAPTER 30 — THE CRISIS OF GRIEF
1. Mark 15:34b, KJV
2. John 14:18, KJV
3. 1 Thessalonians 4:13, paraphrased